The Florida Journals of Frank Hamilton Cushing

Ripley P. Bullen Series

Florida A&M University, Tallahassee
Florida Atlantic University, Boca Raton
Florida Gulf Coast University, Ft. Myers
Florida International University, Miami
Florida State University, Tallahassee
University of Central Florida, Orlando
University of Florida, Gainesville
University of North Florida, Jacksonville
University of South Florida, Tampa
University of West Florida, Pensacola

Frank Hamilton Cushing portrait by Thomas Hovenden. National Anthropological Archives, Smithsonian Institution (Port 22d).

The Florida Journals
of Frank Hamilton Cushing

Edited by Phyllis E. Kolianos
and Brent R. Weisman

University Press of Florida
Gainesville · Tallahassee · Tampa · Boca Raton
Pensacola · Orlando · Miami · Jacksonville · Ft. Myers

All excerpts from the Hodge-Cushing collection are courtesy
of Southwest Museum, Los Angeles, California.

A record of cataloging-in-publication data is available from
the Library of Congress.
ISBN 0-8130-2804-3

The University Press of Florida is the scholarly publishing
agency for the State University System of Florida, comprising
Florida A&M University, Florida Atlantic University, Florida Gulf
Coast University, Florida International University, Florida State
University, University of Central Florida, University of Florida,
University of North Florida, University of South Florida, and
University of West Florida.

University Press of Florida
15 Northwest 15th Street
Gainesville, FL 32611-2079
http://www.upf.com

Contents

Figures

Foreword

Ask any archaeologist what the most spectacular Florida archaeological discovery ever made is, and nine out of ten will say Frank Hamilton Cushing's 1896 excavations at the Key Marco site. Some would certainly argue that the spectacular array of artifacts recovered from Key Marco on Florida's Gulf Coast, including hundreds of unique fiber and wooden objects, qualifies Cushing's discovery as one of the most important in all North America.

In 1900, four years after his fieldwork at Key Marco, Cushing died. He was only forty-two years old. Hailed as a "man of genius" in a memoriam published shortly after his death by the American Anthropological Association, Cushing has in the ensuing century become something of a tragic figure. Some have questioned the authenticity of several of his discoveries, while others have belittled other aspects of his work.

But Cushing is having the last laugh. The publication of Marion S. Gilliland's book *The Material Culture of Key Marco, Florida* (University Presses of Florida, 1975) refocused attention on Cushing and his Florida work, while refuting the old charges of artifact tampering. With the reprinting in 2000 of Cushing's classic report on Key Marco, *Exploration of Ancient Key-Dweller Remains on the Gulf Coast of Florida* (University Press of Florida, introduction by Randolph J. Widmer), Cushing once again has commanded the attention of the archaeological world. His Florida work is being reappraised and placed in its historical and archaeological contexts. Cushing is receiving the accolades he richly deserves.

The present volume, *The Florida Journals of Frank Hamilton Cushing*, edited by Phyllis E. Kolianos and Brent R. Weisman, provides important new information about Cushing that adds to our knowledge of this "man of genius" and his sensational Florida discoveries. The new information comes from several of Cushing's personal diaries that were previously unavailable for study. The diaries cover portions of Cushing's two trips to

Florida (1895 and 1896), including some of the time he was excavating at the Key Marco site.

Though the site at Key Marco has received the most attention, the thoroughly annotated diaries published here promise to refocus attention on Cushing's work at other Florida sites on the Gulf Coast. Aided by the large number of maps, photographs, and drawings reproduced with the diaries, we now have a much more complete picture of Cushing's contributions, including his firsthand descriptions of many important Florida archaeological mound sites.

What makes the Cushing diaries and the accompanying documentation even more valuable is the recent discovery of Cushing's long-lost manuscript on his Florida field research. *The Lost Florida Manuscript of Frank Hamilton Cushing*, also edited by Kolianos and Weisman and published by the University Press of Florida, is a companion volume to this one. Together they offer new data about Cushing's excavations and surveys in Florida. They also provide novel insights about Cushing, an anthropologist and archaeologist who was years ahead of his time.

Phyllis Kolianos, manager of the Weedon Island Preserve Cultural and Natural History Center, and Brent Weisman, University of South Florida anthropologist and archaeologist, have done a marvelous job putting these two books together. Their hard work has not only restored Cushing to his rightful position, it also has given us fresh fodder for understanding Frank Hamilton Cushing and the nature of Florida's Gulf coastal people and environment in the 1890s.

Preparation of this volume was supported in part by funds from the Florida Museum of Natural History's Florida Archaeology Endowment.

Jerald T. Milanich
Series Editor

Preface

Frank Hamilton Cushing, one of the early figures in the development of American anthropology, has for years raised controversy about his technique of participant observation and combining ethnology with the practice of archaeology. The donation of his journals from the Cushing family to the National Anthropological Archives gives an opportunity for further research into and discussion of Cushing's complex character and his professional investigations.

Much of our present knowledge about Cushing comes from his early work with the Zuni from 1879 to 1884, on which he published his research in numerous articles, and his major publication on his Florida explorations, *Exploration of Ancient Key-Dweller Remains on the Gulf Coast of Florida*. Cushing died before he could finish his expansive draft manuscript on his Florida investigations. That manuscript, recently located, will be the subject of a companion volume.

Marion S. Gilliland's books on the Pepper-Hearst expedition give extensive accounts of Cushing's investigations and unique discoveries at Key Marco. It is hoped by the authors that these journals will add depth to those works through these new contributions.

The goal of this volume is to provide new information about Cushing the man and Cushing's research as disclosed in the journals. New information on Cushing's observation of sites on the Gulf Coast should prove valuable to Florida archaeologists and other researchers. Comprehensive annotations of the text are provided in the endnotes in a usable format to guide further research and give an overview of the people and places encountered by Cushing in the wilds of Florida in the late 1890s.

Cushing's journals were written in Victorian longhand with his spelling idiosyncrasies and were carefully transcribed by the authors. The journals give intimate detail of his Florida explorations from May 20, 1895, to June 23, 1895, his first trip, and from January 22, 1896, to May 2, 1896, the

Pepper-Hearst expedition. There is a gap in the journals from March 5, 1896, until his departure from Key Marco on April 24, 1896. Most likely Cushing continued his daily entries in this missing journal that would have related more of his extraordinary Key Marco investigations. Perhaps someday that journal will come to light and can be added to this work.

The introduction reviews Cushing's life and his contributions to archaeology and gives an overview and assessment of the chapters. Chapters 1 through 4 relate the journals and Cushing's daily adventures. Chapter 5 is a synopsis of the lost manuscript, and chapter 6 is a conclusion and summary. Appendices introduce additional little-known Cushing material, including drawings and illustrations that Cushing had planned to use in his research and Florida manuscript publication. This material is located at various institutions throughout the United States.

This volume would not have been possible without the consideration of Robert Leopold, archives and collections information manager of the National Anthropological Archives, who brought to our attention the newly acquired journals of Frank Hamilton Cushing, and the help of many of his staff, especially Vyrtice Thomas, who assisted with needed photographs. Daisy Njoku, media resources specialist, generously responded to our permission and photograph requests.

James Cusick, curator of P. K. Yonge Library, was very helpful in research of Wells Sawyer's papers and the collection of Marion S. Gilliland. Elise LeCompte, registrar of the Florida Museum of Natural History, and Scott Mitchell, collections manager, Florida Archaeology, provided many Cushing documents and artifacts from the Pepper-Hearst expedition. Kim Walters, director of the Braun Research Library of the Southwest Museum, Los Angeles, provided one of the important Cushing journals and many letters of correspondence. Alessandro Pezzati, archivist, University of Pennsylvania Museum of Archaeology and Anthropology, helped tremendously with Cushing correspondence to Dr. Pepper, and Charles Kline, photographic archivist, with important photographs. Deborah Wythe, archivist and manager of Special Library Collections at Brooklyn Museum, provided her excellent guide to the Culin Collection and its rich source of Cushing correspondence and illustrations. We thank also Rip Gerry, collections manager, from the Haffenreffer Museum of Anthropology, for providing numerous Cushing illustrations.

Betty Anholt, John Beriault, George Luer, Salvatore Miranda, and Ryan Wheeler provided very helpful material and information. Joe Knetsch of the Bureau of Survey and Mapping, Florida Department of Environmental

Management, located a map that helped clarify one of Cushing's site names. We also thank the smaller institutions, Tarpon Springs Area Historical Society, Collier County Museum, and Pine Island Historical Museum, for giving very valuable leads and information to further research.

Special thanks to William H. Marquardt and Barbara A. Purdy for their very helpful reviews and constructive suggestions.

Introduction

The Florida journals of Frank Hamilton Cushing provide valuable information concerning his travels along the Florida Gulf Coast in 1895 and 1896. In short but thoughtful entries, Cushing outlines his initial reconnaissance and later investigations of various archaeological sites from Tarpon Springs to Key Marco. They offer an intimate view of Cushing, revealing his constant worries about his health and the many problems and frustrations confronting the expedition. The journals also give specific details about his investigations and finds.

The only known published major writing of Cushing concerning Florida from this era in his life was the remarkable work *Exploration of Ancient Key-Dweller Remains on the Gulf Coast of Florida,* issued by the American Philosophical Society in 1897, three years before his death. The Florida journals give added substance to that book and provide original material concerning the investigations of the Pepper-Hearst expedition.

Through archival research conducted at various institutions throughout the United States, we have drawn together little-known materials produced by Cushing during this period of his life. It is obvious from the tremendous amount of material produced by Cushing that he had every intention of finishing several major works based on his Florida research. This included a lengthy manuscript detailing the geography of the Gulf Coast, detailed accounts of his early 1895 reconnaissance, and the evaluation of artifacts from the Safford and Hope Mounds excavations. Chapter 5 outlines this untitled manuscript (1896e), to be published as a companion volume to this one and titled *The Lost Florida Manuscript of Frank Hamilton Cushing.* Included in this book are numerous Cushing sketches and comparative illustrations created as he analyzed artifacts and formulated major theoretical concepts concerning North American archaeology and ethnology.

Cushing's contributions to science and anthropology have been controversial for more than century. The Florida journals add credibility to his archaeological skills and significance to his ethnographic and archaeological correlations, and demonstrate his independent and intuitive intellect.

The setting of the expeditions was late Victorian America in the 1890s, a time when social progress was fueled by economic prosperity, advancement of science and art, and continued exploration of sparsely settled areas of the United States. Much of fashionable society still was concentrated in the New England and Mid-Atlantic states. The rest of the country resided in various stages of rustic development, except for pockets of venturesome Victorians. America's population, still highly under the influence of British conventions, as evidenced by expositions that staged the advancement of civilization and a propensity for antiquities, began to focus on their vast cultural holdings within America after the Civil War. Romanticism of Native American studies offered an antidote to Victorian society's rather confining lifestyle (Hinsley 1981).

The Bureau of American Ethnology (BAE) was established by the Smithsonian Institution in 1879, under the directorship of Major John Wesley Powell, to collect data on the rapidly vanishing Indian tribes of the Southwest. Powell, very interested in archaeology as well as ethnology, forged early in his department the foundation of the varied field approach in American anthropology, which contrasted with the European historic approach. By 1881 the BAE was actively involved in solving the "Moundbuilders Controversy." Cyrus Thomas, employed by the Bureau, organized investigations throughout the Midwest and South. His extensive report, published in 1894, confirmed that the earthen mounds so prominent on the Eastern Woodlands landscape were the work of the ancestors of the contemporary Native American population (Fagan 1995:32–33). Cultural anthropology was now given a prehistoric past.

In 1879, a young assistant curator at the National Museum was given an opportunity to accompany Col. James and Matilda Stevenson's "collection party" on a visit to New Mexico's Pueblo Indians. Frank Hamilton Cushing's mission was to study and find out all he could about the Pueblo cultures of that region, returning with this information within a three-month period. This was not an idle choice by Spencer F. Baird, Secretary of the National Museum (Brandes 1965:9). Frank Cushing had been with the museum for more than three years and had distinguished himself as a student of American Indians with several papers and an impressive collection of artifacts. The events of Cushing's life that unfolded in the next four and one half years of his Zuni experience, from September 1879 to April 1884, are published by Jesse Green (1979; 1990). This close association with native people left an indelible imprint on Cushing that permeated all other undertakings for the rest of his life.

After Cushing's successful Zuni experience, he enthusiastically mounted a major expedition to the Southwest in 1887 to explore the Hohokam area of southern Arizona. Cushing organized the Hemenway Expedition as an archaeological investigation in which he hoped to use his ethnographic knowledge to interpret archaeological finds. Mrs. Augustus Hemenway, a wealthy socialite, sponsored Cushing's expedition, but months of poor health and repeated relapses finally forced Cushing to relinquish his position in the expedition (Gilliland 1989:41–43). This major disappointment led to later disagreements and accusations over missing papers and charges concerning certain finds.

Frequent illness would plague Frank Hamilton Cushing most of his life. He was born prematurely, July 22, 1854, in Erie County, Pennsylvania. Fortunately, Frank's father was a homeopathic physician, who could give this frail newborn a chance to survive. As a young child, Cushing must have been favored and perhaps allowed more freedom than his siblings to indulge in his natural surroundings when the family moved to western New York. At an early age the artifacts he discovered in the fields and forests of this area intrigued him. He also became acquainted with or aware of the living descendants of these prehistoric artisans as they plied their wares at various local markets. Cushing experimented with different techniques to reproduce projectile points and baskets. His skills and his education developed on the same plateau, a complete awareness of his environment and the intense intelligence to grasp all relevant information. He studied geology, had knowledge of osteology and sociocultural theory (Brandes 1965:8–11).

In 1895 another momentous opportunity for adventure developed for Cushing. Resort areas such as Tarpon Springs, Naples, and Collier's Marco attracted wealthy winter residents and sportsmen to the Gulf Coast of Florida. One of these sportsmen, Lt. Col. C. D. Durnford, was in Naples tarpon fishing and decided to go relic hunting with a friend. Guides took them to a small marl-capped mound on Sandhill Bay (8CR 54) near Naples, where previous disturbance by treasure hunters had disclosed a single skeleton. The thick marl cap impressed Durnford. While he continued to explore the area, his friend Mr. Charles Wilkins went ahead to Marco looking for tarpon. There Wilkins learned of the "muck" basin and incredible finds made by some of Collier's people. Durnford quickly returned from Naples to Marco to examine and hunt for more curiosities. The items found included fish netting and pins, wooden billets and bowls, and carved conch cups. On his trip home to England, Durnford stopped by the University of Pennsylvania to ask experts about his finds. Stewart Culin, director of the Department of Archaeology and Paleontology, and Frank Hamilton Cushing, of the Smithsonian, Bureau of Ethnology, were fortuitously there to examine the objects (Durnford 1895:1032–39). Cushing, chronically ill, was still under the care of physician, Dr. William Pepper, who was also president of the University of Pennsylvania Department of Archaeology and Paleontology. Pepper decided a trip south to further examine the ancient remains reported by Durnford would be good for Cushing's health. This was the setting for the first of the Florida diaries.

As is apparent in the journals, Cushing was eager to begin a new adventure. Even though his health was tenuous, Cushing seemed determined to accomplish this task. It had been years since his Zuni experience, and he languished in Washington still writing up his ethnographies on various aspects of Zuni life and articles on Native Indians for *Johnson's Universal Cyclopaedia*. He had acquired a level of national recognition. In 1881, Cushing married Emily Tennison Magill, whom he now called Emalie, a name derived from their Zuni years. Cushing's adopted Zuni brother, Palowahtiwa, called his wife Em-a-li-a (Green 1990:328).

Six weeks were set aside for reconnaissance of Durnford's discovery and a coastal survey. Cushing bought a new suit, shirts, and hats, as well as a Kodak camera and telescope bag for his journey. This preliminary trip was quickly planned, and by May 21, 1895, Cushing had traveled to New York by rail to board the steamer *Iroquois*. Amusing entries in the diary recount his passage to Florida and note his candid remarks about fellow passengers. This diary ends when Cushing reaches Jacksonville, and another diary begins on a sloop named *Florida* out of Punta Gorda on Tuesday, May 28, 1895.

Cushing's initial exploration of the keys and islands on this trip to Marco was extensive. Many of the place names recorded by Cushing have changed in the past one hundred years with subsequent settlers and increasing development. One of his first stops was at Cashe's, or Garden, Key, where he drew a map of the shell mounds encountered there. The location of this site in the middle of Pine Island Sound was further defined in Cushing's later manuscript. Next stop was Yuzepha [Useppa], where Cushing mentioned many Spanish relics. The following day and again the next week Cushing drew detailed maps of "Beatties" Landing, "a grand shell city," with lagoons, canals, and two burial mounds. These sketched mounds look very similar to the landscape today at the Pineland site complex that is a National Register of Historic Places district (8LL1902) on Pine Island.

Cushing described in detail in his later manuscript the physiography and vegetation of the west coast of Florida in the late 1890s, its geological formation from late Pleistocene into early Holocene, and how ancient dwellers adapted to the land. He also observed the interesting mix of settlers he came in contact with during his southwest Florida trips. These settlers came from many sections of the country and were struggling for their livelihood as farmers or fishermen. Except for a few areas of winter resorts, the islands were thinly settled and thickly overgrown. Cushing seems not to have been shy in approaching strangers or asking for information. These settlers furnished Cushing with much information relating to the inland deposition of prehistoric sites. This further developed his Key Dweller theory and manner of its spread, convincing him of its significance.

Cushing's whirlwind trip to and from Marco continued through the coastal islands and inland: Josslyns Key, Capt. Ellis's Place (Sanibel), Johnson's Key (Mound Key), Demorey's Key, and Naples. He was amazed at the canals, lagoons, water courts, and shell works that he saw repeated again and again in the landscape. Cushing, filled with "great anticipation" upon seeing Marco with Captain Collier, noted some nine canals radiating from the broad peninsula, with three lagoons. The outermost lagoon contained the muck bed of the Durnford and Wilkins's discoveries. Cushing hurried back to Washington to report his finds.

The extraordinary success of the subsequent Pepper-Hearst Expedition began inauspiciously with unforeseen delays in Tarpon Springs. Transportation back to Key Marco was arranged through the University Association of the University of Pennsylvania. This was a powerful support group of individuals who had many connections and interests in the beginning development of Florida. Promoters often provided free transportation to Florida to real estate investors on the steamship lines and early railroads. The association provided Cushing and his crew with travel arrangements south, first by steamer and then by rail, to an affluent little resort community on the Gulf Coast of Florida.

There the schooner for the voyage to Key Marco promised by Jacob Disston, a member of the association, was sponging in the Gulf of Mexico for weeks after the Smithsonian group arrived in Tarpon Springs. When the boat finally returned, Cushing attempted to refit the craft for his expedition, resulting in the *Silver Spray* running aground on a shoal in the river. Continued delays caused Cushing financial problems that continued to plague him over the remaining months in Florida.

Cushing did not remain idle. He surveyed Tarpon Springs and quickly noted the prehistoric presence of past habitation along the Anclote River. Residents steered him to a low, pot-hunted and disturbed burial mound near the schoolhouse. The following weeks were spent excavating this mound and another a few miles north. The artifacts recovered were remarkable. The caches of incised and punctated pottery alone inspired a whole new realm of thinking. Cushing wrote concerning the Safford Mound in a letter to Dr. Pepper dated February 7, 1896, "The discovery of pottery sacrifices each containing five entire vessels of unique form and styles of decoration and a third sacrifice containing three, has literally doubled the value of our whole collection; for seven out of thirteen specimens are such as make museums by becoming at once celebrated the world over when placed on exhibition and published. . . . Clarence Moore's [collection] is not comparable with nor like it save in a limited sense" (Hodge-Cushing Collection, MS.6.PHE.1.20, Courtesy of the Southwest Museum, Los Angeles).

Cushing thought ethnologically; prehistoric archaeology was a means of discovering an older or ancestral style of the living descendants. Although cognizant of the fact that few aboriginal peoples from Florida had survived the European onslaught, he believed all native peoples to be connected. Chapter 6 synthesizes his theoretical views of this connection as a "great arc." Ironically, this concept shares a philosophical premise with such modern legislation as the Native American Graves Protection and Repatriation Act of 1990 (NAGPRA), which has come into conflict at times with modern scientific archaeology over issues of shared group identity and evidence for cultural continuity.

By the third week of February, Cushing finally had the schooner ready to sail toward Marco. He quickly closed down the excavations at the Safford Mound site and ordered the crew aboard. In later years, Clarence B. Moore remarked that the mound was totally demolished (Mitchem 1999:297), though Cushing's continued excavation of the site up until the *Silver Spray* departed raises the conjecture that a remainder of the site may still exist.

Except for one stop at St. James City, the expedition sailed directly to Marco. The muck pond remained as Cushing had encountered it the year before. After dealing with some technical problems of drainage, Cushing laid out a grid system, perhaps the first ever used in archaeology (Widmer 2000:xviii), and systematically began excavating the partially submerged site. Cushing relates ecstatically the daily finds in his diary dated through March 4, 1896. His last entry reads, "Greatest day of my life in exploration." If Cushing wrote the following days in yet another diary, it has disappeared through the years.

Many of the Cushing letters have survived in a rough draft form. He would write at night and then the next day, reread and correct his text. These letters, as fate decided, ended up in the possession of Cushing's brother-in-law, Fredrick W. Hodge, one of his accusers of fraud in the later months of 1896.

Cushing's financial problems intensified by March, as communication with Pepper faltered. An abrupt telegram from Dr. Pepper forwarded to Marco from Tarpon Springs embarrassed Cushing and caused him much anxiety. Cushing's strong reply of March 1 stated that the request for an additional $500 was "small indeed compared with the results," and if the Department felt it could not continue the work that he "must insist on my right as the Discoverer of the nature of these finds, and must seek support elsewhere for carrying the researches on another season. There will be no difficulty in raising ample funds for this purpose" (Hodge-Cushing Collection, MS.6.PHE.1.20).

By March 7 of the following week, Cushing finally received a letter from Dr. Pepper dated February 26, 1896. Cushing then realized that his letters and reports were not being received in a timely manner. This increased Cushing's growing suspicion that he had enemies in the bureau. It was in Cushing's reply of March 7 that disclosure was made of some "startling" discoveries made on March 6 (Hodge-Cushing Collection, MS.6.PHE.1.20, Courtesy of the Southwest Museum, Los Angeles). This date and these finds were also confirmed by the diary of George Gause, Cushing's foreman of the excavation.

On April 2, 1896, Cushing wrote to Dr. Pepper that although they had both been through "deep waters," and though he sincerely regretted adding to Pepper's perplexities, the stay was "amply rewarded." The series of masks Cushing found could stand alone in "primitive religion" and, "in conjunction with the magnificent little figureheads," showed similarities of decoration across several different types of objects. He mentioned how invaluable Wells Sawyer was to the expedition and the need for additional money to continue to retain him (Hodge-Cushing Collection, MS.6.PHE. 1.21).

Wells M. Sawyer's contribution to the expedition was phenomenal. Sawyer's artistic rendering of the wooden objects fresh from the muck captured the vivid paints and character of the artifacts in their original state, especially important now that many have withered and deteriorated beyond recognition. His maps are accurate and his photographs priceless. Perhaps Sawyer's most important contribution was as an educated witness and supporter in his observations to Cushing's discoveries.

Cushing was gratified by Pepper's next letter, requesting a report and illustrations for the Hearst *New York Journal*, as this confirmed the necessity of keeping Sawyer (letter dated April 10, Hodge-Cushing Collection, MS.6.PHE.1.21). Phoebe L. Hearst, wife of publisher William Randolph Hearst, was the benefactor of the Pepper-Hearst Expedition and came to Cushing's support even in the years after the expedition.

On April 14, Major Powell made a surprise visit to Marco. This was the only known visit to Florida by this legend of American anthropology and was the peak of his interest in Florida archaeology. He was astounded by the incredible finds that he termed a "new culture" but told Cushing it was time to finalize and head home.

All the Key Marco specimens were carefully packed and readied for transport. The crew was tired and anxious to return to Tarpon Springs. Irving Sayford, field secretary, and two other crew members, Brady and Clark, had already taken leave on a vessel headed to Cedar Key. Cushing knew that the return trip might be his last chance to compile as much data as possible on the key dwellers. The entry dated Friday, April 24, 1896, describes several keys and islands that the expedition explored on its return voyage.

Using St. James City as a base for several days, Cushing and crew (Emalie stayed with the Whitesides) mapped, photographed, and tested sites in and around Pine Island and Charlotte Harbor. George Gauses's diary, also included in this volume, helps fill in the places visited as the Cushing diary entries became sporadic.

One of Cushing's goals was to photograph the shell wall on Demorey's Key. After Cushing's death, Clarence B. Moore claimed this shell wall was not prehistoric, but of Spanish origin. Sawyer defended Cushing's observations in a rough draft intended to correlate with Cushing's unpublished manuscript. Major Powell paid Sawyer in 1901 to compile all of the Cushing manuscripts for publication. This did not materialize because of Powell's death in 1902.

There is confusion about the last stop made by the Pepper-Hearst expedition prior to its return to the Anclote River. After Cushing passed the lighthouse on Egmont Key, he stopped at the quarantine dock on Mullet Key, now known as Fort De Soto Park, at the entrance to Tampa Bay. This key has changed extensively from its configuration of a hundred years ago. Cushing's journal described threatening weather and his decision to seek safe harbor in the mouth of Mullet Key. According to his Florida manuscript and Wells Sawyer's rough draft, they actually sailed southeast to the mouth of the Manatee River where it empties into Tampa Bay, arriving about four o'clock that same day. He explored and mapped a site on the south bank now known as Shaw's Point (included in the De Soto National Memorial) and claimed that it represented "a complete confirmation of reef and key theories" because of its resemblance to keys of the lower coast.

As the *Silver Spray* passed Hog Island near St. Joseph's Sound on its way to Tarpon Springs, Cushing lamented not being able to stop and investigate the burial mound there. Moore did in his 1903 season in Florida, stating that although the mound had been woefully dug into, "it was completely demolished by us" (Mitchem 1999:297).

Cushing avoided reporters on his return to Washington and by the end of July traveled to a retreat in Maine. In a small colony of cottages called Haven (now part of Brooklin, Maine), Cushing began the monumental task of writing up the Florida expedition. Maj. John Wesley Powell rented one of the cottages and had arranged for stenographers to assist Cushing. Although not included in this volume, the important portion of a Maine diary concerning Florida revealed the daily log of dictation as Cushing produced page after page of manuscript in neatly typed half-page segments with his handwritten corrections. Portions of this effort became the basis of the report on ancient key-dweller remains given at the American Philosophical Society Proceedings in November 1896. The rest of the manuscript, which totaled some 1,000 pages, was never published, because of Cushing's sudden death in 1900 and Powell's death in 1902. A synopsis of the largest portion of this manuscript (some 708 half-pages) appears in chapter 5. It contains many intuitive Cushing observations that helped establish his theoretical thinking, as well as his brilliant perception of now commonplace archaeological techniques.

While in Maine, Cushing was involved also in another project, experimental reproduction of native items. This life-long hobby became a focus to help furnish the "new" museum of the Smithsonian soon to be built, the National Museum of Natural History. His contributions of skillful workmanship included bark baskets, trays, scabbards, celts, and battering stones. Cushing was recognized as the pioneer in experimental reproduction, a modern technique in archaeology. Most of the keynote speakers at Cushing's memorial—the 305th meeting of the Anthropological Society of Washington, April 24, 1900—refer to this innovative methodology of research. W. J. McGee remarked that Cushing was "a master of manual genius," with an application peculiar in that "his efforts were expended in interpreting inventions by others rather than in making inventions of his own." Powell's address spoke of Cushing's experiments and workshop of technological investigation that culminated in his paper "Manual Concepts: A Study of the Influence of Hand-usage on Culture-growth." Alice C. Fletcher described the key to Cushing's character as "an unconscious sympathy" that dominated his personality in all of his relationships, as she quoted his address in 1895 before the American Association of the Advancement of Science:

> Well-nigh all anthropology is personal history; even the things of past man were personal, like as never they are to ourselves now. They must, therefore, be treated and worked at, not solely according to ordinary methods of procedure or rules of logic, or to any given canons of learning, but in profoundly personal mood and way. If I would study any old, lost art, let us say, I must make myself the artisan of it—must, by examining its products, learn both to see and to feel as much as may be the conditions under which they were produced and the needs they supplied or satisfied; then, rigidly adhering to those conditions and constrained by their resources alone, as ignorantly and anxiously strive with my own hands to reproduce, not to imitate, these things as ever strove primitive man to produce them. (*American Anthropologist* n.s., 2, 1900:368)

Controversy and Cushing are synonymous. Through the years the Cushing persona fluctuates in acceptance. In recent years it has even been acceptable in the anthropological community to lampoon photographs of him posed in native clothing and to ridicule his methods. What was the true character of this man? Some perception of his character becomes possible through his writings in the following journals. They reveal Cushing's personal frustrations and aspirations and his attitude toward others, and served him as a reminder of communication written and received. The diaries are not scripted in Cushing's noted flowery speech. These tiny, 3¾" × 6¾" journals that concern the Florida expeditions span the time period from May 1895 to May 1896. No doubt other journals were written on a habitual, almost daily basis, as Cushing recorded meticulously the weather, his surroundings, and the day-to-day events. The diaries give the reader a sense of time and place.

The journals are reproduced verbatim, except for the modern usage of "ss" in place of Cushing's "sf," and capitalization and punctuation are added for easier reading. Cushing used word spellings prevalent in his time that are now considered secondary or obsolete. At the end of several journal entries, Cushing closed with cryptic messages that remain undeciphered. These messages appear to be a type of phonography or phraseology shorthand popular in the nineteenth century. These cryptic messages are reproduced and discussed in Appendix B. He often left out vowels, especially when entries were hurried. His penmanship reflected his mood. Sharp, crisp-scripted letters and words portrayed confidence, good health, and enthusiasm. Anxiety, illness, and exhaustion were exemplified in often illegible written words.

Several personality traits are discernible in the journals. First, he was still a man trying to prove himself to his professional contemporaries. Jesse Green (1990:358) wrote that Cushing was considered by many of his associates to be "too gauche" to be properly professional. The first diary of May 1895 reveals Cushing totally delighted during his passage to Florida that one of the fellow passengers knew of his previous explorations in the Southwest. This was not a pompous reaction, but a simple, candid response. In Victorian America, a person's appearance was almost as important as his or her background. Prior to his journey Cushing outfitted himself with the attire befitting a gentleman from the Bureau of American Ethnology. Cushing strove to be acceptable.

Second, Cushing loved the adventure of fieldwork. Much has been written of his early years and his passion for nature. The diaries set the tempo of Cushing in the field . . . and not in the field. In the field, Cushing is full of energy and vitality. He laments with deep regret on the return voyage from Marco not being able to do further investigation because "Emalie and all the rest are worn with it all!" Not in the field, Cushing has constant headaches and physical ailments; he can barely work. In Maine, Cushing used his experimental learned skills to reproduce Indian objects as a release both out into the field and as recreational therapy. One passage, dated August 28, 1896, states, "Had slight headache early, but pecked stone and worked up some spruce root which relieved me."

Those characteristics could fit any number of people. Yet Cushing was different. Often he was called strange. His perception was fine-tuned through his prior experience and observation, as he viewed ethnology and archaeology as a continuum. The paradox of Cushing was his attempt to live in two worlds, Victorian America and America's First Peoples. He strove to fit into Victorian society, but his heart returned again and again to the elements of nature and the landscape of the native peoples. His was a dual nature, for he saw the world through the eyes of a scientist and from within traditions of his adopted people. Cushing had the unique ability to cross the boundaries of his own culture. His actions perplexed many of his contemporaries and antagonized others.

At the time of Cushing, much of archaeology was about the gathering of relics and antiquities to satisfy the curiosity of the "enlightened age" about the prehistoric and "primitive" past. This research implicitly acknowledged that Progress would inevitably obliterate the American Indian and all the tribes of the Native American past. Cushing was fully a part of an American anthropology racing to salvage evidence of American Indian cultures through ethnology and archaeology. But he wanted more. He was searching for a unified theory in which all artifacts could be viewed as expressions of the aboriginal mind. He wanted to comprehend not only how an object was made, but also how it was connected to other objects and to a larger cultural system. Cushing writes concerning the Safford Mound site, "But it was not merely in material remains that this place proved rich. The observations I was able to make during the progress of the work formed data so significant that from them many customs and much of the sociologic and governmental organization of its builders can be clearly made out" (Cushing 1896a).

The concept of settlement pattern or landscape archaeology has become a regular feature of modern archaeology. Cushing was one of the first to see the value of this approach, as he correctly visualized the terrain and the constructed earth and shell works as patterns of the adaptation process along the west coast of Florida. At one point he climbed as high as he could for a bird's eye view, so he could draw maps of the mounds, canals, lagoons, and watercourts. The concepts of settlement clusters and spatial patterning of site systems were fully understood by Cushing and figured in his theoretical thinking. The settlement patterns were repeated over and over throughout the coastal landscape as far north as the Manatee River. In some sense, Cushing was a pre-processualist, as elements of his thinking resurfaced years later in the New Archaeology of the 1960s.

In the months after the expeditions, Cushing strove to complete his manuscript as revealed in many letters to Dr. Persifer Frazier, secretary of the American Philosophical Society. In one letter (Cushing to Frazier, dated February 8, 1897), Cushing wrote of censure from the society resulting from the fraud charges (1897a). Stress was apparent in Cushing's increased illnesses and unfulfilled promises.

The diaries and the "lost" manuscript introduced in chapter 5 make a compelling case to rethink Cushing. Native Americans can view a mature Cushing, not the obtrusive Victorian of his earlier years, but someone aligned to their perspective and appreciative of their culture as the unified foundation of humanity in America. Anthropologists can revel in Cushing's continued ethnological epistemology as reflected in all aspects of this archaeological expedition. This book opens the door to valuable new research and information for archaeologists and archaeological theory. Numerous landscapes and archaeological sites, many unrecorded, are identified as they existed one hundred years ago. Examination of Cushing's theories compared to the processual and post-processual movements could fill another volume. In memoriam to Cushing, H.F.C. ten Kate remarked, "Cushing was not a savant, a man of much book-learning. The book in which he read was Nature," and if he (ten Kate) had not "passed through the school of Cushing," he would not have fully comprehended his future investigations (ten Kate 1900). The astute readers of this text will acquire new information and indeed pass "through the school of Cushing"; the reward is a new insight into the mind of one of American anthropology's true original thinkers.

1

Adventure and Initial Exploration

From the University Hospital in Philadelphia, Pennsylvania, a former patient, Frank Hamilton Cushing, boldly penned his name and his mission. Thus began in the late 1890s an archaeological odyssey of exploration on the west coast of Florida. The following transcribed journals relate the passage to Florida of the initial exploratory trip undertaken for preparation of the planned expedition to Key Marco. The first diary in this chapter, although only a few pages, revealed the eager anticipation of Cushing on a new adventure.[1] The second diary detailed his first reconnaissance on the southwest coastal islands and keys of Florida, and chronicled his explorations of late May and June 1895.[2]

Frank Hamilton Cushing
U.S. Ethnologist, Bureau of Ethnology,
Smithsonian Institution,
Washington D.C.
University Hospital, Philadelphia, Penna.,
20th May 1895
   Itinerary of trip to Florida undertaken by advice of Dr. William Pepper for sake of health and for explorations in S.W. Gulfcoast region, in the interest of the Department of Archaeology, University of Pennsylvania.

Monday, 20th May 1895
   Went yesterday in the afternoon, to Mr. Hovendens[3] restful old place at Plymouth Meeting to visit a few hours with my dear Tennison.[4] Was well all the evening, visiting mostly with her, but spending the hours of dusk with family and visitors—Mr., Mrs., and Miss Sears (editor on Times) and Mr. Doyle (the sculptor) and wife, and later Doctor & Mrs. Carson of Norristown.

We returned at about ten o'clock and visited so very happily a long time before sleeping. The air was sweet and the night sounds of nature mostly. We slept perfectly and awoke quite well between six and seven. We were too late to get 8:20 train, but reached the 9 o'clock train in time and roded [sic] in with Mr. Hovenden to Broadstreet. Thence we went to "Johns" and bought—suit, blue serge ($12.00) pair shirts for outing (3.00) tie (.50) and Telescope bag (1.30 or 50) and at Allens (hatters) of the derby (yesterday) a soft knock about hat for my trip, the two 5.50.

Called on Rau the Photographer and he filled me out with Kodak camera and nice lot of instructions.[5] Also called at Eakins Studio and got knife which he had kindly sharpened. Went to call, then, on Messrs. Kreamer, Dunn and Krhumber of the Land Company. They had kindly procured as had written, passage (not includ[in]g state room and meals) on Clyde Steamer "Iroquois" sailing tomorrow (Tuesday May 21st) direct for Jackson-ville;[6] also pass partway on Plant system railways to Punta Gorda. These Mr. Kreamer handed me with letters of introduction (additionally to those already sent to [blank area]).[7] He gave me points about boats, trips to Marko [sic] and Colliers, to Pine Isld and up river to Kissim[m]ee to Great Mound beyond Ft. Thompson.[8]

They were all most courteous in good wishing and good byes. Joining Emalie[9] at Wanamaker's then went up to Culin's[10] where she staid to lun-cheon and I went on to hospital where Miss Featherman gave me a sumptu-ous luncheon (for me!) I then went to call on Doctor Pepper,[11] and was but little delayed. He is very greatly interested and hopes for great results, ulti-mately, of my reconnaissance. I hope truly too. He handed me one hundred and fifty dollars ($150.00) on account of University and opened formal acct. Asking itinerary and vouchers when practicable. Wanted as much of collection as possible, inclusive of human remains crania and the like. De-ferred giving further instructions until five, at University; but told me of great expectations of Land Company if this proved successful for next au-tumn and winter's work under my direction.

Then went up to Culin's and was joined by Emalie who accompanied me to hospital and helped pack trunk and telescope; latter for steamer. We first bought ticket and arranged for baggage transfer to steamer satisfactorily. Were in the midst of packing when Dr. Pepper came. He was brusque and very solicitous about my care of self and gave minute directions about food, drink, medicines, and regimen—about not over working etc.

Emalie left me soon after and I remained, supped finished packing and awaited transfer people who did not come until nearly eight o'clock, but

Fig. 1.1. Advertisement for the Clyde Steamship Company. By permission of Tarpon Springs Area Historical Society.

then took down both pcs. Meantime Dr. Newton got medicines and pulled bread, vienna loaves etc.—enough apparently for a month, but I suppose not. They were all nice. Supt had been instructed to await pay. All good wishes including patient next door. Reached Culin's half past 8. Went out with him and got some memorandum books; then came home and retired with Emalie. Another of these beautiful night talks ere we slept. Read a fine letter from Brinton.[12]

Tuesday, 21st May 1895

I awoke this morning and visited awhile with my dear Emalie, and then for an hour or so, slept & rose at seven or a little before and went down to arrange for transfer of remaining baggage; a large telescope-bag of bread (pulled, Vienna loaf, and graham) having been sent by Dr. Pepper. Also went to Jeager place and Wanamaker's; but neither open. To tobacco store and got papers gem, pouch and matches ($1.45). Bought 2 pr. cuffs, 4 collars, & returned at little after eight. All at breakfast and well, and happy. Culin off to Dr. Pepper's from whom there was a letter emphasizing his instructions and sending anti-malarial medicine. It was fine courtesy. Made ready at half after eight, and bade my dearie and the rest God's blessing and goodbye. Culin accompanied me to station. Took 9:50 train & seat in Parlor smoking car—only one vacant. Had splendid table and was absolutely well. Wrote letters to Culin, Emalie, Eakins, Drake, and Mr. Eger thanking him & associate for courtesy of pass.

On reaching New York went to S.S. Wharve and fixed all the baggage. Then went to call on Judge Daly but found him out.[13] Then to St. Denis to dine (1.10) & wrote Emalie again. Bot [bought] magazine, ink & little ink bottle filler, then took elevated for steamer which sailed at quarter of four. Found one of best staterooms ("E," upper night hand deck) for which & for meals had to pay $10.00, 50 cents to waiters & 25 to baggage boy.

Thereafter wrote mema & exp accts., cut magazine, ate dinner and wrote & read. Raining hard as it has all day and is chill, quite rough too but this far not sea sick, & well still.

Wednesday 22nd May 1895

Slept restfully and well last night. Still raining and colder in morning. Was looked after nicely by my porter a West India mulatto of pleasant manner and pleasantly accented speech. Am not quite well, but far from sea sick or badly off otherwise. The wind higher and the sea rougher. Meals good, although lunch of cold meats not wholesome; hence fell back on my pulled bread boiled milk and extra eggs. Saw dolphin and little after noon

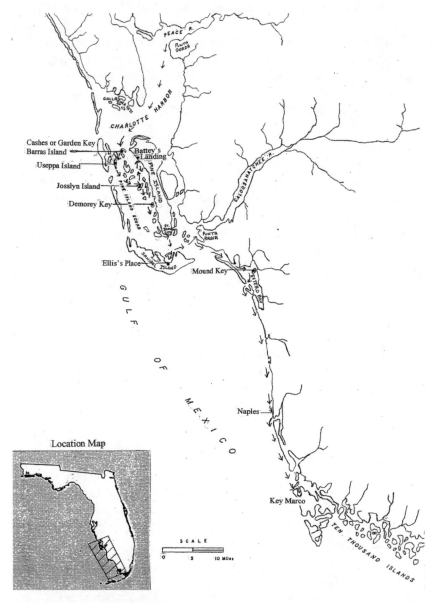

Fig. 1.2. Location map of southwest Florida showing Cushing's initial travels in 1895.

sighted light of Hatteras, and later head lands low lying, sand & forest covered.

Met couple of men—one Superintent [*sic*], other Secretary of a Phosphate mining company. Secretary a graduate of Harvard and quite manly as well as bright. Quite taken with me. The Supt. a dry humored quaint Central New York Yankee—combination of Keam and Livingstone in appearance with a stilson laugh (like a good natured whinneigh). Met by shake introduction a Mr. Goff who hails from Albion [NY]—Proves to be so called scapegrace son of old Mr. Goff who had the garden below Uncle Ezra's.[14] He has boated the entire gulfcoast of Florida, and has given me valuable information of practical nature. Late in day met young man named Tresk— Engineer who had seen service in Mexico, New Mexico and Arizona. Was telling me of "Cushings" wonderful explorations down there and was wild when he learned I was the man.[15] He also has proven very helpfully disposed, and invites me to his place, Belleview, in central part of state.

The morning has cold, the evening clear and stars are coming out, boding better tomorrow—Bed at 10:30.

The journal entries stop at this point in the first diary. Cushing arrived at Jacksonville on the Clyde Steamship line on May 24, 1895.[16] He traveled up the St. John's River to Sanford, and then by rail "through the pinelands and tropic lowlands of Florida" to the little town of Punta Gorda located on the Peace River that flows into the gulf on the west coast.[17]

*   *   *

Cushing began another diary on May 28, 1895. In this diary he describes his explorations of the islands, bays, and keys of the southwest coast of Florida in detail, along with maps. Cushing must have used this diary as reference, as these are the sites he described at length in his presentation to the American Philosophical Society in November 1896. Some of the many places Cushing visited are: Casey (also Cashe's or Garden) Key; Useppa; Josslyn's Key; Demorey's Key; Battey's Landing on Pine Island; St. James City; and Ellis's Place on Sanibel Island. On Mound Key, or Johnson Key, Cushing encountered not only "great groups of mounds," prehistoric canals, and lagoons, but also abundant Spanish remains, as he did at Useppa. This diary tells of his meeting with Captain Collier on Key Marco and of seeing the "great shell settlements" with "abundant surface relics." Cushing's dissatisfaction with his first hired crew and their indifference to his mission is obvious in this diary.

Tuesday, 28th May 1895
    Left Punta Gorda 7:30 P.M., in Sloop Florida, Captain Smith & Man (Thomas Parkerson).[18] Reached mouth of Charlotte Harbor 11 P.M. & anchored.

Wednesday, 29th May 1895
    Off at 4:30 A.M.—past Gallaghers and numerous other Keys to Cashe's Key (shell city & first encountered canoe ways),[19] at about 10 A.M. After lunch to Yuzepha [Useppa] Key: Beautiful spot. Many relics mostly Spanish. Spanish keeper, very accomodating [sic]. Fish Camp of Smith Bros. Mght. [sic].[20]

Thursday 30th May
[Cushing explored Josslyn's Key in the early morning.][21]
    Beatties Landing where very Grand shell city and lagoons and canals occur, also two burial mounds at 10 AM.[22] Fish camp lunch time. St. James City night. Captain Whiteside most courteous, and had prepared for me.[23]

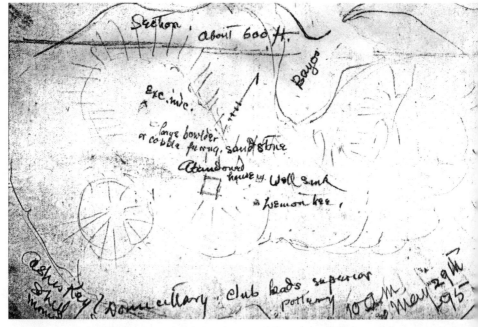

Fig. 1.3. Cushing's sketch map of Cashe's Key, May 29, 1895. He labels the great shell mounds "domiciliary" and notes the superior club heads and pottery. An abandoned house with a well and various tropical trees are remnants of an early settler. Courtesy of Southwest Museum, Los Angeles, Hodge-Cushing Collection, MS.6.PHE.2.1.

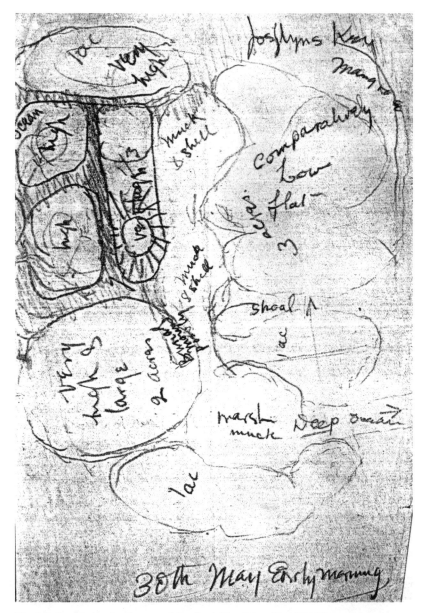

Fig. 1.4. Cushing's sketch map of Josslyn's Key, May 30, 1895. He outlines the high-to-very-high mounds, giving approximate acreage of each mound site. Cushing indicates a burial mound in the center of the sketch. Courtesy of Southwest Museum, Los Angeles, Hodge-Cushing Collection, MS.6.PHE.2.1.

Friday 31st May 1895

Left Capt. Whiteside's at noon P.M. Sanibel Island at 1:30. Rode a craft to Gulf—Thre[e] Sisters' place of Barnes & daughters with young Dunlop [sic].[24] Back at 4 to N.E. side of Isld., Capt Ellis' place (picturesque primitive palmetto thatch) where found bank conches canoe way (small) and mound (small originally shell, turned into burial).[25] Decided to anchor & sent for by boat. Dug and found skull also parts of two other skeletons.

Saturday 1st June 1895

Resumed digging at 7 A.M. Got parts of five more skeletons and skulls. No relics. Left 11 A.M. Punta Rassa 2 1/2 PM. Schultz totally indifferent.[26] Estero Bay night.

Sunday 2nd June

Bad night. Hot, rain, mosquitos, diarrhoea, bad food, worse sailors (indifferent about progress). Went 7 AM to Johnsons (Mound Key). Once Great Aboriginal Shell city with distinct canoe-ways and canals. Johnson and wife very crude but good.[27] Some relics shell sinkers, stone maul pot-sherds trials at photos. Spanish remains abundant. Back 10 AM. little wind. Storm brewing Capt. unwilling to proceed. Lying here at anchor. Headache.

[Two entries for June 2, 1895; Cushing must have decided to elaborate about the day and explorations of Mound Key.]

Sunday 2nd June 1895

Up at five this morning. Squally with calmes. Mound Key at 9.30 wonderful place. Frank Johnson very civil wife also. Both rude but good. Gave me maul and "plummets." Willing I dig or examine all please. Took photos (five or six). Mounds in three great groups like shell cities. One 60 ft high hundred long 75 or 80 broad.[28] Truncated. Domiciliary. Canals & lagunes leading to and between all. Sand burial mound to east abundant pottery & remains. Back to boat at 11. Not under way until two. Men slow & indifferent or miskil[l]ed. Reached Doctors pass nevertheless. Grand storm clouds. Fairy scenes. Gathered shells on white beach. Capt Smith killed heron. Fine eating. Discovered huge turtle. Turned her. Walked beach awhile. Retire at nine. Rain, heavy, but mosquito[e]s not so bad.

Monday 3rd June 1895

All up very early. Captn butchered and took quarters of poor turtle. At breakfast fine eating better than steak which is like. Tried to make start but

men afraid. Provoking. Laid until at least half past nine. Came out in nearly
a calm. Progress poor until wind freshened at about 11. Then so good that
at 12 reached Naples. Presented letter to Captn Large, Fine man.[29] Beautiful
place. Large showed ancient canal—straight, nearly mile long. Unquestion-
able. Fine relics found in her. Must return. Have free permission to dig, as at
Mound Key.

Under way at one. Fine breeze, later storm of rain & wind. Sea rough but
reached Marko pass at four, Colliers bay & place at five Capt Collier very
civil (but bursting with irreligion). Has superb shell cut netting, sinkers,
stool! Carribean [sic] in type very willing for digging; probably keen, but
most civil and interested beyond question.[30] Will show me about in morning. Raining, but cooler, am writing in cabin. On this place outside. It is
"The Tropics." Immense camps all the way in, too. Have great anticipation.

Tuesday 4th June 1895

Rained all day. Went about with Captain Collier seeing great shell settlement on his own and Capt Cuthberts place. As extensive as any I have seen,
and has abundant surface relics. About fifty acres in all with at least nine
canals leading radiatingly from waters of the broad peninsula occupied to
centers of groups (of irregular size and with at least three lagunes 2 small &
one very large, through which canals communicate).[31] The outermost of
lagunes small and muck bed where the Wilkins and Durnford finds were
made. Covered with water surface and brackish backed up by tide. Great
prospects; and despite water shall excavate tomorrow with two men. Captn
Collier very courteous and invites me to dine with them tonight. Has also
several men and offers to take me out to numerous sand mounds. Have
milk and venison brot [brought] in today. Very close evening and more
mosquitos than ever saw before.

[At Marco]
Wednesday 5th June 1895

Up very early. Bright morning. Took camera & Smith & went ashore between half past 6 & 7. Took numerous views of canals & lagunes—in particular one to excavate, fortunately water little lower. Had man before eight.
Located place for him and had turf dam made within which to work.[32]
Smudged countless mosquitos, after which not difficult to work. Found
place to dig for self. Smith Helped! We struck relics almost immediately
and found from time to time all day. Worked myself with men until six PM.
Splendid success. Captn Collier went off on business & has not returned.
Night not so warm; but mosquitos & sandflies worse. Breeze late.

Thursday 6th June, 1895.

Settled accounts took some photographs & set sail north at about eight. Good wind and made fine progress. Wrote and slept in cabin nearly all day, ill with severe headache. Reached Punta Rassa at 6 o'clock.

Friday 7th June 1895

Up at four, having written until nearly one, mosquitos & sandflies being very bad. Set sail at once eating breakfast under way. Reached St. James City at little after 6. Captn Whiteside just up. Determined to discharge sloop and men. Mean set, both. Paid, unladed & sent off. They took razor case, & promised to return extras. (Afterward learned that pious dolts did nothing as promised).

Made arrangements with Captn Whiteside, to go out exploring Keys the morrow. He was very nice. Gave me room in "Johnson" cottage & made me at home to meals in his own. Rested, wrote and washed up things rest of day. Visited evening. Terrific thunderstorm during afternoon little hail. Much cooler. Explored two shell mound sites one very interesting 1200 yards long, high straight East of "City" other dug away; conforming to shore. Pottery & bone.[33]

Saturday, 8th June

Wrote letters, provisioned; got skiff from Captn Smith & secured services of Alex Montgomery, & set sail for Josslyns Key & Bettie [sic] place at about half past 10. Reached Josslyns 2 PM. Had meal. Photographed. Dug in Main lagune. More shells, less muck than at Marko but similar in other ways. Quite rich. At four set sail for Beatties. Reached there at sun set; Kirk there & hospitable. Pleasant evening. Slept in onion room with three flea bitten dogs. Rested ill.

Sunday 9th June

[Blank area, then Cushing listed places and dates visited as a reminder.]

3rd arrived & spent 4th & 5th June at Marco. Latter in digging. 6th June sailing to Punta Rassa which reached at night fall. Sailed over to St. James City in early morning 7th June. Most hospitably received by Captn Whiteside and given room in Johnson cottage sent sloop home. Went to explore mounds off right of place morning, left with Captn afternoon. Both very long, low, marginal—one removed. 8th June started to Beatties Place with Mr. Montgomery in Capn Smiths little sail boat.[34] Stopped at Josslyne Key & excavated in muck. Rich. Reached Beatties evg for supper well rec'd by Mr. Kirk.[35] 9th Excavated all day with indiffe[re]nt luck. 10th Most of day

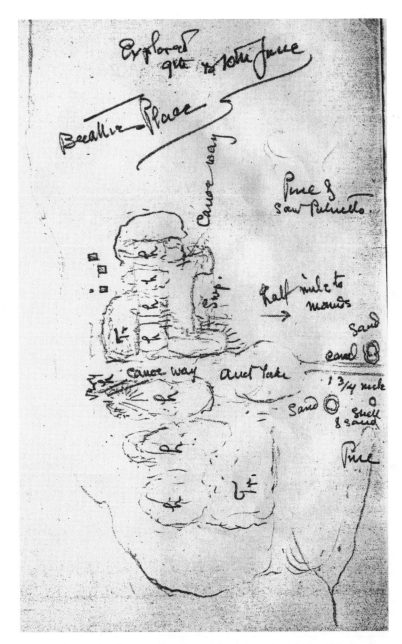

Fig. 1.5. Cushing's sketch map of "Beatties Place," June 9 and 10, 1895. On this map, Cushing shows the numerous high and truncated mounds, canoe ways, and the ancient lake. To the right he draws the double-topped mound now known as the Adams Mound. Courtesy of Southwest Museum, Los Angeles, Hodge-Cushing Collection, MS.6.PHE.2.1.

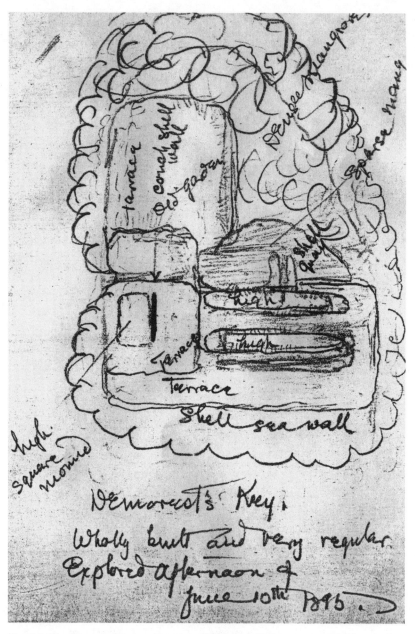

Fig. 1.6. Sketch map of Demorey's Key, afternoon of June 10, 1895. Cushing clearly outlines the high mounds and terraces, and he draws an arrow to the bold line indicating the artificial conch shell wall. Courtesy of Southwest Museum, Los Angeles, Hodge-Cushing Collection, MS.6.PHE.2.1.

visited by Captn Whiteside & "Dick" & visited sand mds & canals. Monday (11th) excvted all day until 4 then pulled up camp & ventured via Demory's Key to St. James City.

Sunday 9th Work & return evg St James

Monday 10th leave Smith & Montgy Keys work at Demory's.[36]

Tuesday 11th Return from Keys

Wednesday 12th Camp at Ellis md & wk
[This day Cushing stayed in the palmetto shack that he described in detail in his unpublished manuscript.]

Thurday 13th Return from Sanibel & lecture evg.[37]

Friday 14th leave St. James City

[One last entry occurred in the back of the first May diary, Thursday, 23 June 1895, written as Cushing traveled back to Philadelphia.]
Thursday 23rd June 1895
    Up at seven, looked after by my porter, slept in upper berth last night, and better still. Very bright and something of southern balm in air, but with indications of clouding again. Had a good breakfast and am much better again. Have spent morning writing diary—letter to Emalie, and memoranda.

2

Excavations amid Anxiety

Cushing and his entourage arrived at Tarpon Springs by railway the first week of December.[1] The arrival of a Smithsonian expedition to this small city established in 1887 must have caused some excitement among the residents. Cushing soon learned that the schooner promised to him by Jacob Disston was on a sponging trip in the Gulf of Mexico. He secured from Messrs. Cheyney and Marvin comfortable lodging for his group at a cottage on the grounds of the Tarpon Springs Hotel owned by Hamilton Disston and Associates.[2] Leandro Safford, adopted son of the late Anson P. K. Safford, one of the founders of the town, directly approached Cushing concerning Indian remains on some of the Safford property.

Within a few days, Cushing quickly surmised the presence of rich archaeological sites along Anclote River and the burial mound on the Safford property.[3] His enthusiasm and curiosity about the prehistoric peoples of Florida could not wait, and he decisively set about excavating the Safford Mound.

As days turned into weeks, the *Silver Spray* finally returned home by December 22 only to run aground on a shoal in the harbor.[4] Meanwhile, Cushing hired a crew for the Marco trip and to work the current excavations he had undertaken not only at the Safford Mound, but also at the Hope Mound, some miles north of the Safford site. On December 11, 1895 the Safford Mound excavation was under way,[5] and by December 20, the Hope Mound, a smaller site, excavation began under the supervision of Wells Sawyer.[6]

Cushing thought he was almost finished with the Safford Mound excavation by January 22, 1896, and busily cataloged the finds, restored pottery, and made preparations for the pending Marco expedition. He was very concerned about the many delays to his true mission and especially about the expenses incurred. Yet, the Safford Mound was extraordinary in splendid pottery designs and in its more than six hundred skeletal remains.

Cushing hardly hoped to find even finer relics in the shell settlements of southwest Florida. The Safford Mound excavation continued for almost another month, until February 23, when the *Silver Spray* finally set sail.

The following portion of the journal dated "22nd Jany to 4th March '96," relates Cushing's anxieties, recurring illness, and difficulties in proceeding to Key Marco. The townspeople of Tarpon Springs befriended him and were instrumental in his ultimate success.

Wednesday, 22nd January 1896

Awake a[t] 6 not withstanding lateness of retiring. Wrote on paper before breakfast, tho, not well. After breakfast lent sharpie to White & Richie.[7] Began cataloguing with Sawyers assistance. Dizmally bad day and none of us well, save Emalie. Storm brewing. Dreadfully upset by difficulties in way of my duties. Broken into by Mr. Cuneva of Tampa, correspondent.[8] Couldn't give him regular interview, but told him quick story & turned him ov'r to Sawyer. Mr. Safford called few moments. Catalogued alone nearly all afternoon and all evening. Mr. Sayford marked. Have nearly finished Safford Mound Colls. including skulls and skeletal remains.[9] Thunderstorm all evening. 12 to bed very tired. [cryptic message; see Appendix B]

Thursday 23rd January 1896

Up at half past seven after early awakening and sleep again. Head bad from weather and continually worse until evening. Slightly better now but has sadly interfered. Went down to mound. Early Gause had found plummet. Extreme W. edge. Nearly filled in. Came back to breakfast, then went to cataloguing again. Finished skeletal entries and began on Hope Mound. Worked all evg tho sick. Took calasaya but ineffectly. Paid off Richie, White, and Styles.[10] Allen acct. also made out. Bot br[an]dy & Ext! Not useful. Mr. Sawyer better. Work greatly hindered by heavy rain (with thunder). Bed after 12 slightly better.

Friday 24th January

Up at little after six, but attack of gas so bad had to lie down again. Resumed cataloguing immediately after breakfast and continued all day. Had Clark and Gause up to assist in laying out Hope Colln. Fairly dry by afternoon, and got classified and catalogued in the main. Been growing better all afternoon. Unable, however to do other writing, except little this evening. Skulls nearly all packed and work so well on as to be in way of finishing by Monday. Paid Allen today, 15.50. Wishes to go still. All worked

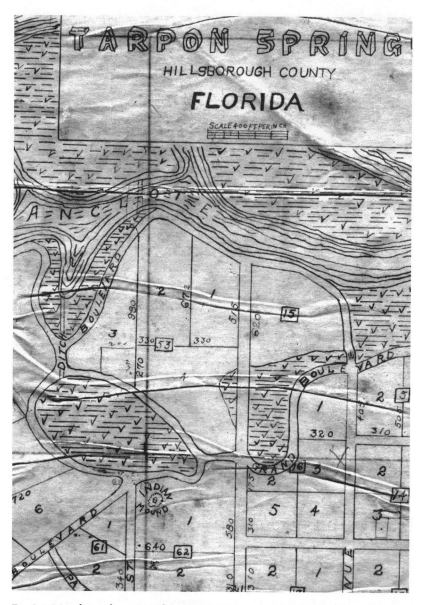

Fig. 2.1. Map drawn by J. B. Walton in 1883 showing Indian Mound. By permission of Tarpon Springs Area Historical Society.

Fig. 2.2. Cushing repairs vessel from Safford Mound at a cottage on the grounds of the Tarpon Springs Hotel. National Anthropological Archives, Smithsonian Institution (Port 22a).

hard today and all tired. Some splendid sherd finds this afternoon by Gause. Fine day and night. [cryptic message; see Appendix B]

Saturday 25th of January 1896

Up at six 30 feeling quite well. Very bright morning but soon clouded and in afternoon rained. Luckily had all outside material classified and catalogued, and continued at same until evening inside house. 465 odd entries a finer and greater collection than had thought.[11] Had applications from young men named Saunders and Whitehurst today. May take Saunders. Don't like Whitehurst. Paid Gause ten dollars. Got from Mr. Cheyney dozen beers today. 1/2 doz day before yesterday. Wrote Mr. Ledyard last night sent this morning. Ready for bed at 11:30. [cryptic message; see Appendix B]

Sunday 26th January 1896

Up at seven and at once at work restoring jar. Cooler but clear today. Mr. Bergman, and to some extent Mr. Sayford worked at classifying sherds from the Safford. Mr. Sawyer developed more plates;[12] I worked on altho: very ill all morning at pot restoring save whilst recv'g application of sailing mastership of boat from young Whitehurst which refused and talking with Mr. Richie abt newsletter. Prof. Smeltz came and took Sawyer off to his island abt noon.[13] Better this afternoon. Emalie too. Worked until near midnight restoring bowl, vase, and large water jar. They are fine. Mr. Safford came in and watched while Mr. Cheyney also looked in. Bed at half past one Belles. [cryptic message; see Appendix B]

Monday 27th of January 1896
Up at seven. Very bright but cool day. Went about for boxes after breakfast, but had all been taken so set Clark, Bergman, and Sayford at making new ones of old. They made excellent progress. Had Gause and Allen work at mound. Allen filling in, Gause digging at SE sector. He found skull of adult and remains of child and found other skeletons. Went on with restorations. Completed vase and little bowl remains. Both maskoidal in most interesting way (Fishface man mask).[14] Had most reassuring letter from Dr. Pepper this evening.[15] [cryptic message; see Appendix B]
Was only fairly well. Cloudy tonight. Bed at one. Had Allen prepare paper pulp for more vessels which shall complete tomorrow.

Tuesday 28th January 1896
Up early again but not so well. Continued restorations, and had men continue as yesterday. 2 at mound and 3 making boxes of which now seem to be enough. Got 1 [d]z 3 b[ee]rs from Mr. Cheyney. Five to come. Worked until late, then went out with Emalie and Mr. Sawyer to look at one of the most glorious moonlight scenes down by the Bayou we have any of us ever beheld![16] Bed nearly one as usual.

Wednesday, 29th January 1896
Up at six, and at work on pot. Suffering ag'n from a severe diarhoea [sic] and hard work to keep about; but saw to packing skeletal remains, to having mound continued (burial of interest discovered but not much else) and restored form of large jar to completion also little cup and roughed out gem of bowl. Do not feel happy tonight but suppose it is illness and weariness. Mr. Clark in from Anclote for excuse from duty on acct. of death of Old MailCu [?]. Had application this morning from young Mr. Hudson to go with me. Not to bed, until after midnight again. Cool, cloudy.

Fig. 2.3. North view of the Safford Mound excavations. National Anthropological Archives, Smithsonian Institution (FLA 137).

Thursday 30th January 1896

Up at six not feeling wholly rested, but at work at once on large jar smoothing and on little ewer building. A brilliant summer morning went down and got more glue also bottle of venice turpentine and Emalie's waitch [sic] at Express. Had mound work continued with one man, Clark and Allen go for moss and Bergman and Sayford pack.[17] Met Antonio Gomez and engaged him as Skipper at $30.00 per mo.[18] Finished all save decorating on the three pieces. Messers Safford and Sawyer joined in nice walk during evening. Bed at 25 of 12. Warm night and a little cloudy.

Friday 31st January 1896

Warmish day low clouds and much smoke from prairie fires. Had Mr. Sawyer go on with mound work (to cov'r as much as possible of it and he found just at night a nest of pots two drumo (1 tapering cylinder other elongated gourd shape) two pots and broken but fairly complete four lobe ves-

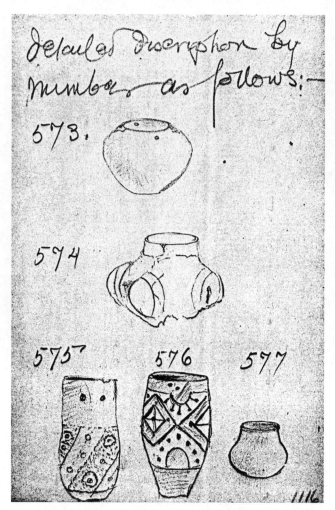

Fig. 2.4. Cushing's catalog sketch of Cache I, Safford Mound. National Anthropological Archives, Smithsonian Institution (MS 2527).

sel.[19] The ware is superb—the finest yet found in Florida. Worked all day on restorations. Not very well part of day, but worked well. Packing progressed admirably. Will have S.E. sector of mound thoroughly worked up now.

Saturday 1st February 1896
    Up at six. Very sweet morning, but day grew warm and close. Packing kept on until dark and bulk of collection now finished. Sent Sayford and Bergman to minstrel show. Sawyer and Emalie did not care to go. Went on

Fig. 2.5. Lithic points from the Safford and Hope Mounds. National Anthropological Archives, Smithsonian Institution (FLA 131).

with restoration work. Also made some Armenian cement which works well.

Drew money ($50.00) today. Dischg'd and paid Allen; also Clark and Gause. Worked at bowl tonight with grav'g tools bot mostly from Mr. Fowler. Sleepy but better. Thank God.

Sunday 2nd February 1896

Up at before six but came back and slept until seven. Very warm and quite windy with oppressive air. Not stres[s]ing but at work all day finishing up rest'ns. Bergman packed Sawyer mad[e] photo studies of spec'ms.[20] Mr. Cheyney called and saw new finds was now greatly impressed. Engaged two men—Shemley and Hedges for trip and work here. Miss Gause gave me Arena today.[21] In it read to Sawyer and Emalie. Made tools of old files etc bot last night of Mr. Fowler too.

Raining quite hard. Had boxes covered.

Fig. 2.6. Safford Mound Cache II in situ. National Anthropological Archives, Smithsonian Institution (FLA 116).

Monday 3rd February 1896

Up at half past six somewhat ill, very nervous and blue. Worked hard at arranging for renewed work on the mound, with Gomez engaged and un-excelled sailing master and to have Silver Spray brought up. Hudson and Clark to help. Engaged young Hudson and Capt. Brady for crew. Paid VanWinkle bill. Finished restorations. Another discovery of pottery nest—one long gourd jar, one lobed gourd jar, one large olla and an exquisite picked line and curved jar.[22] Photoed by Mr. Sawyer also important sherds. Mrs. Olney came in with Mrs. Wharton Smith. Negroes here. Worked cementing new finds.

Tuesday 4th February 1896

Up at 6:30 very much depressed. Still cloudy yet warm morning. Out to mound early and had excavations continued along Sawyer's lines.[23] Many fine sherds but not much else. Went to get boxes and packing material. Finished cooking pot. Showed collection to Mrs. Troutman and her sister Mrs. Wharton Smith again. Got Livery bill—23 dollars. One item too large. Had Hedges work 1st time today. Silver Spray stuck on bar but beteterd [sic] tonight. Went down to count berths, will have to leave out a man or two. Brady and Hudson came. Ordered water aboard. Gomez good. Dr. Reed came tonight showed collection to Mr. and Mrs. Marvin.[24] Later to him and Mr. Cheyney. Better 12 m-.

Fig. 2.7. "Contents of the second general pottery sacrifice," Safford Mound. Collections of the Anthropology Division of the Florida Museum of Natural History.

Wednesday 5th February 1896

Up at six but returned and slept until half p[a]st seven and better for it. Had boxes arranged for marking as there was heavy rain. Cleared up and got more boxes. Got groceries for Spray and arranged with Gomez to water and clean her. Had mound worked on but with small results. One unique adze and sherds however, practically completed cataloguing tonight & settled some bills. Bed earlier very high wind and heavy rain again. Close weather but better.

Thursday 6th February 1896

Up at 7 after long but disturbed night's sleep. Very high wind and heaviest rain yet. Was exceedingly harassed today by untoward events and reports of Prof. Smeltz about Gause. Saw Rickards, later his testimony was not conclusive. Wrote more catalog. Settled drug bill, carpenters & painter's bill, Livery bills of Vinson Fowler and Dickinson.[25] Sayford exps., and Bergman salary. Had visit from Mr. Wharton Smith and Mrs., and Dr. Reed this morning, from Dr. Reed this evening. Men at work on mound. Portions of bowl and pot recovered. Engaged Hedges. Arranged to discharge Stanley and Prince. Got canvas for tarpaulin. Worked at catalog evg. Worked out totem mark on pot & Whyte [White] painting.[26]

Friday 7th February 1896

Up at half past six. Fearfully blue. Went down to mound and had men fill in—Discharged poor Stanly [sic]. Am sorry chose Hedges in his place. But he was very good about it. Came up and went to get Druggist sundries and settle printer bill and choose paper. Then hunted scraper which at last found. Discharged Prince. Arranged to have trays made aboard Spray. Filled out more catalogue. Had talk with Mr. Cheyney. Had couple of visits with Dr. Reed one this evening with him and family. Very pleasant. Worked up pile decoration as totemic necklace and navel [Cushing sketch] shell gorget with Sawyer.[27] In better mood but worried dreadfully. To bed earlier. Betwn 11–12, after writing Dr. Pepper & Col. Kreamer.

Saturday 8th February 1896

Was up at six not well and not able to do all I wished; but sent Bergman to mound, finished catalog, had boxes arranged for special specimens which am leaving out as long as possible for Mr. Disston by Dr. Reed's wish. Went to mound and directed NW corner worked. Went to Spray and arranged for storage of provisions etc and for crew. Found matters very shipshape. Had trays made. Came back and with Captn Gomez arranged for rest of outfitt[in]g, and with George for provisions all of which save for selves now ordered. Very very tired. Very hot moist day, and tonight heavy rain. Went over to hotel to hop[e] in order to satisfy demands of people here. Am asked to address them but hardly care. Home early and to bed. Paid Brady 10, Gause 5, Dorsett 5, Sawyer 7.

Sunday 9th February 1896

Up very early with bowel sickness but came back to rest and at last sleep until nearly.eight. Not able to do much of anything during morning except choose some boxes and write a little in catalogue. Visit from Dr. Reed who wished to take me out to Lake Butler.[28] This he did after dinner, late, we being accompanied by Mr. Sander and Misters Cheyney and Safford. Returning re[a]d and then wrote whole evg to Dr. Pepper.[29] Am a little better to night. Has been cold out partly cloudy today and as windy now and much colder. To bed in fairly early time.

Monday 10th February 1896

Up at six 20. Superb morning. Feeling much better, but nearly worn out with men and offers. Discharged Hedges etc. Went down to Spray to look over storage, after seeing Captn and ordering down bulk of provisions. Got alabaster & gypsum & dolomitic pendants (Gause and Dorsett at work) at mound as passed.[30] Arranged for bad times a cast net, etc. etc. Worked little on both catalog and Pepper letter. This afternoon had pleasant visit with Dr. Reed and arranged for talking with Mr. Disston about contng work. He is favorable. Mrs. Levis offered to give us tents, bedding, utensils etc. & to fix up cabin she and Mrs. Inness.[31] Mr. & Mrs. Safford called tonight want me to go up river. Prof. Smeltz talked great deal and like self tonight. Have been very well but hard worked.

Tuesday 11th February 1896

Up this bright morning before six with same trouble, but better as day wore on and no headache. Went with Mrs. Levis after breakfast, to select tent, matress [sic], bedding, utensils, which she kindly turns over to the Spray for our work. Went down to Spray to arrange with Captn what her and Mrs. Inness have their way in fixing up cabin. Too much taken as I found this evening after returning from trip down river with Dr. Reed. Many traces of Anct remains opp. mid., and on bluffs everywhere below. Trip arranged for tomorrow with Dr. Reed to Gulf shore. Up to see abt bill, but unable. Had corners of Md excvted by four men today. Many sherds some important. Bed early.

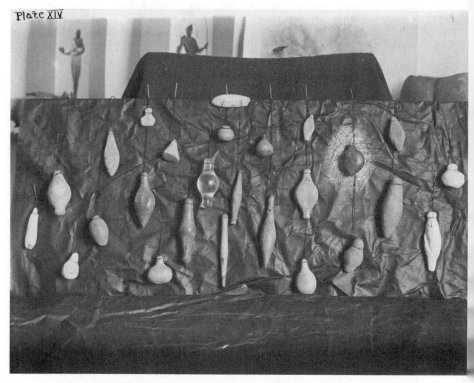

Plate XIV

Fig. 2.8. Plate 14, showing plummets from the Safford and Hope Mounds. Collections of the Anthropology Division of the Florida Museum of Natural History.

Wednesday 12th February 1896

Up at six laying down a little after then up and about to breakfast, when called by Dr. Reed in loud singing. Had early breakfast, went to mound, got more of face jar,[32] then returned and with Doctor & Mr. Sawyer went down to neighborhood of Seaside exploring Cheyney and Indian Island where immense nos of flakes, spalls, blades occur then Stony point & Indian Island.[33] Camps nearly swallowed by sea indicating recession of coast.[34] Got 2 knife & one flake blade and one superb dart point. Home at 3 pm very tired. Down to examine find 2 pots and vase for cooking all in SW edge very near surface.[35] Wrote some Mister Cheyney. Paid Hudson 4.00 Clark 5.00. Bed early to rest. Warm possibly storm tomorrow headache better.

Thursday 13th February 1896

Up at six or little before. Fairly well. Packed charts etc., in preparation for loading Spray. Received word Gomez was ill by Brady. Went down after breakfast with Dr. Reed. Break bone and liver. Saw Mr. Cheyney and arranged to postpone payment of hotel 2.00 per day for each. Drdful but all's well that ends well. Loaded from noon on with buckboard the tide being reported rising sufficiently. High enough nearly today. Had some pleasant visits with Dr. Reed today, & others all very kind. Two pendants. Closed excavtns and ordered all aboard for tomorrow.[36] Very hot day rainy tonight. Bed early woefully tired.

Friday 14th February 1896

Up at six. Filled catalog up to date, and went out to arrange alot. Tray for specimens and Spray boat. Load at half past eight. Had load taken down (raining lightly) and then boxes stored in rear of bank, as freight agt. was

Plate XV

Fig. 2.9. Plate 15, types of pottery from burial mounds. Collections of the Anthropology Division of the Florida Museum of Natural History.

not able to give any satisfact'n. Mr. Safford very kindly helped and gave me chart case. Got steamer to try to taking Spray off but alas stuck her on rocks, but had sent Bergman Sawyer and Sayford aboard, noon sailed around with Commodore after dinner & have tried all afternoon to get steam'r to take out tonight.[37] Paid George (cook) 15.00, Dorsett 5.00 Hudson order. Went down tonight with Mr. Cheyney, Boys grumpy & in partly came home, went to Founder day entertainment with Emalie, and came in to read Miss Gause's arena & bed early.

Saturday 15th February 1896

Up at six. Rain and chilly. Went out to ship with Dr. Reed early. Captn better and again dosed him and gave him glycer supstory [sic] with effect at last. Drew hundred dollars and paid Gause ten. Got beers and sent down to Captn. Boat taken off rocks last night and moved to bend this evg. Had two or three visits with Dr. Reed today and with Mr. Safford. Made lead, casting in sand. Went to boat again and ordered poled beyond MacElroys if possibl[e] high tide tonight. Still rainy and dizmal but warmer. Bed at about 11 with bad taste but better hopes. Mr. Disston coming!

Sunday 16th February 1896

Up at six very ill with facial headache. Took crotine and slept little; but was not much better. Went down past bayou saw Spray about t'was last night. Little later went down with Dr. Reed who prescribed calomel triturate for me.[38] Afternoon worse. Went for bill, but not ready. Came back more ill. Visit from Dr. Reed & Mr. Safford. Visited Spray. Sawyer anx to arrange extension.[39] Had Brady order poles got from Sponge Harbor. Captn better. Slept betwn 4 & 6. Better for it. Went down to arrange with Captn Patten abt moving Spray abt skiff and abt life preservers.[40] Visit from Mr. Lewis and the Saffords. Evg bed soon after—11. Mr. Disston came but I dnt see him. Clearing.

Monday 17th February 1896

Up three times during morning, with headache; not finally until half past seven. Colder and not clear until noon. Got some things at drugstore—Ponds and calomel triturate 35 and 50 cents, also bill from Mr. Decker. Dr. Reed and Mr. Disston called. Latter much interested. They proposed walk later and we with Misters Safford and Saunder went down to Donaldsons on Gulf and past Black Sink. Found camp, also bits pottery at sink. Spray not moved last night only little. Could not visit her today but saw Captn

Patten & he thinks cant be moved for 3 or 4 days yet. Sad business. Think
Mr. Disston inclined to help me so hope will.

Tuesday 18th February 1896

Up at seven, and breakfasted at half past. Then went down to boat.
Moved again about 600 yards. Started intendg to make exploratn up R.R.
track; but trouble aboard detained Cook and men at loggerhead's, may
mean dismemberment again. Did all could to settle and ordered spar for
Dinkie [sic], shelves in cabin, typewriter table all fixed up.⁴¹ Cabin put to
rights beautifully. Sawyer & rest of party proper well. Plan to send party out
if matters not mended tomorrow. Came home and wrote. Got accounts together. Bills all fearfully large. Got oars & staples. Drugs also. Tired out in
afternoon and laid down. Better at night read and wrote again. Bed little aftr
11. Still cold and not promising fair or good tides.

Wednesday 19th February 1896

Up at 6, and wrote on catalogue until breakfst time, then on memoranda.
Very overcast with usual result on self, but cleared later, and went to find
Mr. Safford to pilot ship for afternoon. Met both him and Mr. Disston who
was very pleasant. Went to boat. All well, but trouble again about meals.
Had to make a rigid rule for party specl'y. Arranged to take boat out at full
tide by pole & tug. At time got oars and saw & stand of wood. Then went
out with Dr. Reed to boat. She was taken about a mile and agen [sic]
stranded on bar nearly opposite Murphys. We landed and found mound
(probably) near (up from) Murphy place which we crossed marsh to and
found a vast camp (of ages), met Mr. Murphy an author & not uncultivated
gave me one of his books (on hunting) and full permission to dig.⁴² Will try
tomorrow. Crossed over to Bryens Mill.⁴³ Dr. found spearpoint & lance and
rasping stone showing grind work use. Home in calm (boarding Silver on
way to F bro. bill bad. Home at six. After dinner long talk with Mr. Levis.
Mr. Safford in for medicine, little left to buy. Emalie worried over acct, I in
turn. Fearful night headache. Dr. Reed gave me bronxmine.⁴⁴ Mr. Disston &
Gause's wife sent flowers.

Thursday 20th February 1896

Letter from Dr. Pepper asking reports—late last night. Up with headache
but crotine and rubbing bettered. Up at eight. Book on Florida from Mr.
Disston returned to Dr. wants to join me in explorn next winter and asks to
stay here but cannot. Went down river to Spray with Dr. Reed accompanied

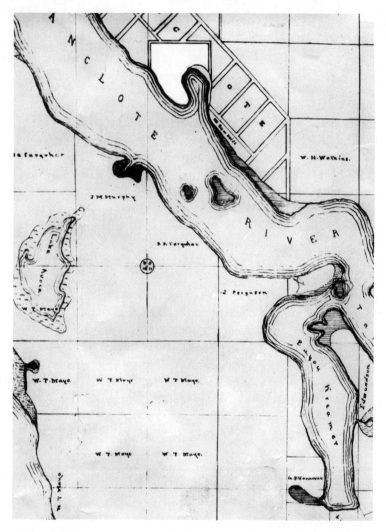

Fig. 2.10. 1884 map drawn by J. B. Walton shows Murphy's land and sawmill across the Anclote River. By permission of Tarpon Springs Area Historical Society.

by Mr. Disston & a Mr. Gilmore. Visited Murphy mound again and Deserter's Hill.[45] It is a noble wood & place, and beyond near Lake Avoca undoubtedly rich in ancient remains.[46] We found abundant chips. Returned in time for late dinner. Met Steamer on way to take Spray off for which she succeeded in doing. Returned and worked at bills & accts. reports etc. Kept busy till late, yet had some lovely visits with various friends in evg with Mr. Safford among others.

[For Doctor Pepper] — List of Photographic
Blue Prints of Excavations made
and types of the Specimens collected in Burial
Mounds near Tarpon Springs Florida

Plate I — Subsidiary Village-site mound, typi-
cal of smaller Burial mounds.

Plate II — Extended mode of mound-burial.

Plate III — Brushed mode of mound burial.

Plate IV — Dismembered mode of mound burial.

Plate V — Bunched or communal mode of
mound burial.

Plate VI — Pottery-grave burial in mound.

Plate VII — Symbolic or figure-disposition of pot-
sherds in general mortuary sacrafice in mound.

Plate VIII — Figure disposition of pot-sherds in
special mortuary sacrafice in mound.

Plate IX — Types of crania: a, showing war-club
marks; b, showing hole healed at edges, possibly
trephining; c, showing excessive asymmetry;
d, showing os tnea (solitary example.

Plate X — Arrow and knife points.

Plate XI — Large dagger and knife blades.

Plate XII — Large dagger or dirk blades ⅓ natural size.

Plate XIII — Axes and adzes of diorite; Two showing haft and wedge-polish.

Fig. 2.11. List of photographic blueprints Cushing sent to Dr. Pepper. By permission of Haffenreffer Museum of Anthropology.

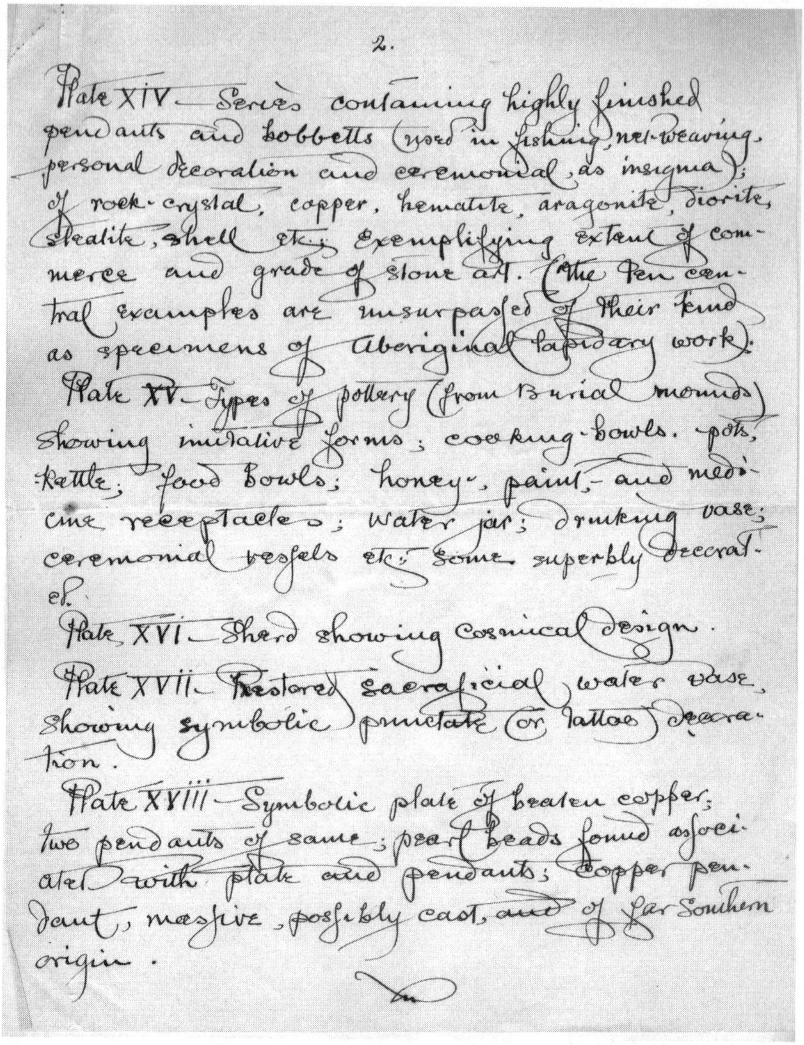

Plate XIV — Series containing highly finished pendants and bobbetts (used in fishing net-weaving, personal decoration and ceremonial, as insignia); of rock-crystal, copper, hematite, aragonite, diorite, stealite, shell etc; Exemplifying extent of commerce and grade of stone art. (The ten central examples are unsurpassed of their kind as specimens of Aboriginal lapidary work).

Plate XV — Types of pottery (from Burial mounds) showing imitative forms; cooking-bowls. pots; kettle; food bowls; honey-, paint-, and medicine receptacles; water jar; drinking vase; ceremonial vessels etc; some superbly decorated.

Plate XVI — Sherd showing Conventical design.

Plate XVII — Restored sacraficial water vase, showing symbolic punctate (or tattoo) decoration.

Plate XVIII — Symbolic plate of beaten copper; two pendants of same; pearl beads found associated with plate and pendants; copper pendant, massive, possibly cast, and of far Southern origin.

Fig. 2.12. Second page of blueprints. By permission of Haffenreffer Museum of Anthropology.

Friday 21st February 1896

Up at about half past seven. Hazy day, by no means well. Went during morning to see Mr. Disston. He at first offered to give or lend 5.00 but backed down. Then to stand for hotel amount, was dreadfully disappointed. But concluded to draw on Dr. Pepper or consult to seek aid of Mr. Lewis. He advised drawing on strength of letter of Jany 24th. Was very kind and helpful. Wrote Dr. Pepper quite asking this time specialing letter.[47] Finished it only at two of morning (copying by foot). To bed fairly well however, very much relieved by Mr. Lewis suggestns. Everyone lovely to us about going away and with good wishes. Were I less determined, would despair.

Goo[d] weather promised and hope now Spray is free to leave tomorrow.

Saturday 22nd February 1896

Up early and well, but of course blue. Hoping to get off, but despite letter written, the bank affair to manage and others to write. Acted on Mr. Lewis suggestn and mad[e] draft (for 60 days) on Dr. Pepper, for $500.00. Mr. Safford made all easy for me and even offered 1000 same terms. Noble fellow—settled drug bill, livery & paint bill. Hotel bill (personal portion; tried to get reduction; but no use). They are mean about that. Altho splendidly helpful at first. Didn't have to use Mr. D's name. Wrote Dr. Pepper again that hadnt drawn etc.[48] Wrote Gill about Sawyer enclosing his letter. Wrote Captn's. Whiteside and Collier. Sent also labelled plates of collectns to Dr. Pepper. Brady and Hudson up in sharpie. Sent all heavy luggage down in her. All well aboard. Ordered crew ready 11 tomorrow as couldn't get away. Worked till midnight on correspondence & copying. In evng, went to Disstons with Dr. Reed & Mr. Safford. Mrs. Disston pleased with photos & anxious to make expd next year. Bed late. Both of us far from well. Arranged with Side pak launch tomorrow & asked them to breakfast.

Silver Spray Sails to Key Marco

Finally, on February 23, the *Silver Spray*, packed and ready, began its voyage to Key Marco. Cushing, ill again, continued to finalize arrangements. Many of the townspeople and good friends that the group made came to see them off, and by late morning the schooner was under way. Sawyer eulogized the bon voyage with an appropriate poem of their coming explorations on the mangrove islands to the south.[1]

Besides Cushing and his wife, Sawyer, Sayford, and Bergmann, the crew of the *Silver Spray* consisted of Capt. Antonio Gomez, George Gause, Thomas Brady, Alfred Hudson, Robert Clarke, Frank Barnes, George Hudson, and George Dorsett.[2] George Gause also kept a diary of the trip to Key Marco and the day-to-day happenings. Portions of that diary that correspond to Cushing's journal are reprinted in context.

The short trip with a stop at St. James City had some heavy seas. Cushing was irritable and very eager to hear from Dr. Pepper, but no mail. On Wednesday, February 26, the *Silver Spray* reached Key Marco and anchored offshore at the back of Collier's fine new hotel.[3]

By early the next morning Cushing was at the site, and he immediately set to work. All illnesses disappeared, and his spirits soared. The importance and excitement of the remarkable discoveries in his now hurried entries are apparent. His inherent ethnographic methodology continued, as his overview of the ancient shell city and its inhabitants remained most prevalent in his thinking. This portion of the following journal related the trip and the initial excavations and finds.

Sunday 23rd February 1896
   Up at little before six—suffering wretched headache. But was little relieved and enabled to sleep some (until after seven, by Brady Crotine and

by rubbing). Emalie not well either, but we were nearly packed and at breakfast by eight—the Saffords with us. After breakfast got soda, headache powders (45 cts worth) extract beef (2.90) and whiskey for emergencies (2 qt.) Also meat from Steward, Paid 1.00 to waitress, 1.00 to head waiter, 2.00 to Steward, 25 to boy & 50 to Anson. Packed & carried things down to launch which Mr. Safford made ready at ten. Mr. Disston, his little boy and girl; Mrs. Inness, Mr. Lewis; little Ray; all came down to accomp[an]y us; Mr. Cheyney & other friends to see us off and Mr. & Mrs. Safford. Was not well at all and not visitable. Mr. Disston wanted to have me get mast Colliers. Wants to go to Yucatan next season & to have me return soon. Dr. Reed too (he came down).

Reached the Silver Spray at 11:15 all well. Good wishes of all. Under way at once. Good crew. Fearfully sick on way but worked putting to rights. Fine Speed. Beautifully sailing boat. Evening meal better. Sawyer read poem. Bed at 10 opposite Mullet Key with good breeze.

Monday 24th February 1896

Up at quarter of eight after having wakened early. Captn ferried watches and sailed all night. Opp. Egmont, in morning rather light breeze. Not very well, but worked all day putting cabin to rights and making hammock for Emalie who saw a spider and hen[ce] to be provided for with other sort of accomodatns. There is no longer anything but evil fortune for me on this exp. Sfd [Sayford] doing nothing, others dismal, but crew splendid. Was some ill tho not much. I love the sailing, but ah! how hard! Passed Boca Grande and nearing Sanbal [*sic*] Light. 1:30 very weary. Brady sick & medicated. Captn better. Warm and cloudy, breeze fresher. Gulf beautiful.

Tuesday 25th February 1896

Up at six feeling very wretchedly having worked so long at hammock and worried so much. Spray had anchored of Sanybel [*sic*] at 3 and got under way daylight with NorEast breeze. Came to anchor inside Sanybel light at 7. Bright Sun. Green keys and isl[an]ds all around. Wonderful waters. After breakfast set forth in Sharpie with Emalie and whole party for St. James City.[4] Brady & Clark sailing heavy seas & much spray. So sick laid down in peak. Slept little. Reached St. James City abt 10:30. Captn Whiteside calm; slow about setting me orders but courteous. Saw Captn Smith & sons.[5] Hospita[b]l[e] sent Barnes—the Missus Whiteside & so on. Hotel open.[6] Beautiful to get back, but so worried. They like others only one or two of reports. No very important mail. Came back afternoon. High wind heavy sea wait till morning to sail. Clear, cool. Hammock done made perfect with Capt Tonys help.

Wednesday 26th February 1896

Up early and altho at first ill, better speedily. Not quite right however, all day. We were under way at sunrise with fine norwest breeze. Swell quite heavy. Had shelves in commissary Dept. begun. I set Mr. Sayford at catalog which he has wholly neglected of late it seems. Set other men to making bags, and put boat to further rights. We turned in to Colliers Big Marco Pass at about 2 o'clock and anchored to rear of Colliers fine new hotel. Went ashore at once with Sawyer. Called on Captn Collier. Not at home, but Mrs. Collier there. She was very cordial and said digging would be free to us & welcome. Came aboard after looking at the muck lagoon (which is as I left it last spring) and went up bayou to a point of white beach. It proved to be the edge of ancient shell city of enormous extent. Canals and lagoons wondrously distinct and interesting second only to Colliers and undoubtedly as rich.[7] Grand at dusk. Late home, then Emalie who continues ill & I called on Captn Collier. He was most affable. Back at 9:45. Even sea birds here communal & organized. All have leaders siget.[8]

Thursday 27th February 1896

Up very early. Had ship cleared & boxes sent over to shore. Fairly well; but both Emalie and Mr. Sawyer not at all well. Warm but threatening yet beautiful day. By eight o'clock at diggings—old lagoon. Got gutter to carry off water and boards for burrow way from Captn Collier. Had water baled out from old hole, and work extended toward bank. All intreating pile dwelling. Pile laid bare,[9] whetstone, shell cups, shell pick (axe) with handle complete, skull, baling scoop, pottery shells, beautiful bone and ivory hair pins found.[10] An assured success!!

Fig. 3.1. Cushing's sketch of shell axe and baling scoop. National Anthropological Archives, Smithsonian Institution (MS 97-28).

Etc. Sawyer began plan, but taken ill evg.[11] Emalie and I better. Spent day at digging. Evening working. Pale & rain tonight. Bot 2 buckets, sieve, venison.[12] All good crew, save Hudson ill too.

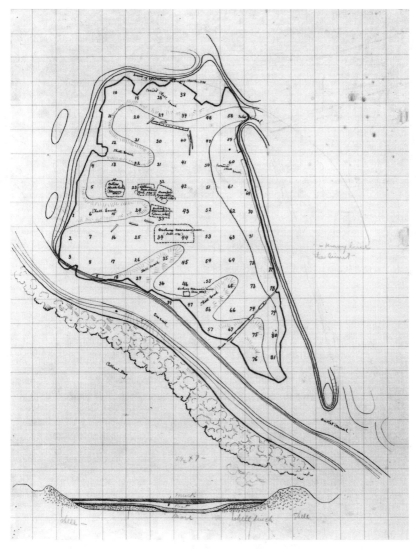

Fig. 3.2. Map of Key Marco drawn by Cushing, showing grid system and earlier excavations. Brooklyn Museum, Culin Archival Collection. Cushing Collection [6.3.026]:A143.™

[Cushing wrote Pepper about this day.]

George Gause, one of the crew members from Tarpon Springs, began his diary on February 26 as the boat arrived at Marco.[13] Excerpts from that diary relate to Cushing's writings and confirm the same excavation recoveries. The diary, reproduced as written, also revealed Gause as an invaluable

Fig. 3.3. Bone pins from Key Marco. Collections of the Anthropology Division of the Florida Museum of Natural History.

member of the expedition with his suggestions, attitude, and work ethic. On February 27, Gause wrote, "27th got up in morning went to work in the mamoth cove got the some ivory some bone & two pots one scull and a little connio [canoe?]. Venison for supper gone to bed all is well and lonely."

Friday 28th February 1896
    Up at half past six. Quite well and Emalie better; but Mr. Sawyer under the weather still. Had Captain & mate fill water and get wood. Then went down to peat-lagoon with all hands. Finds began immediately tho storm last night had filled holes more than half with water which had baled out. During morning found shell club—bowl nearly entire & parts of other; Double headed billet; single billet. Blade of carved paddle. Many fine shell specimens. Rain set in furiously at noon but later all went back & made wonderful finds, skull and nest of wooden bowls, trasp billets and idol,[14] carved deer horn handle and symbolic button in form of anglefish [sic] superbly carved.[15] Three perfect and two nearly perfect shell cups, others unfinished. Worked till dark. Capt. Collier has offered shak [sic] for storage. Move around soon as can. Bot rope for sharpie. Rain all afternoon and tonight.

Fig. 3.4. "Idol" from Key Marco collection. University of Pennsylvania Museum, Philadelphia Accession No. 40914, Neg # S4-147118.

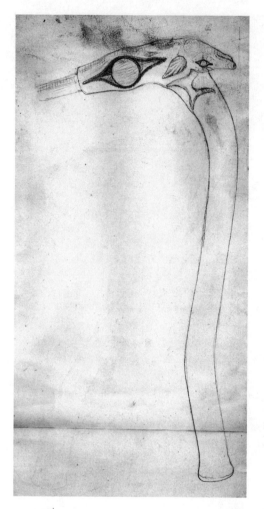

Fig. 3.5. Cushing's sketch of carved adze handle. Brooklyn Museum, Culin Archival Collection. Cushing Collection [6.3.005]:267.

Saturday 29th February 1896

Slept fitfully, having retired too early, but rested. Was up at six and breakfasted at seven. We were all off for the water court by half past. Found it flooded. Had to make two great troughs, make a ditch thro shell bank, get buckets, 3, and set force to baling.[16] Emptied by half past eleven, had Hudson's find (two bowls, a little image, mortar and pestle, little pestle, and double headed pulper) photographed, then took up.[17] Afternoon more baling than excavated. Got board, toy canoe, two superb conch dippers, netting, club handles & heads, bone dirk, (Bergman) floats, thatch (palmetto)

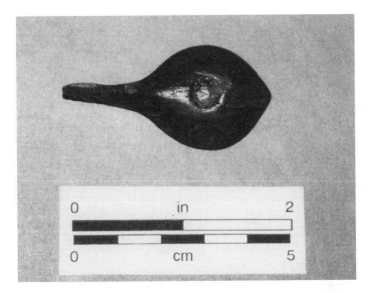

Fig. 3.6. Carved angelfish button from Key Marco. Collections of the Anthropology Division of the Florida Museum of Natural History. FLMNH Cat. No. A5600.

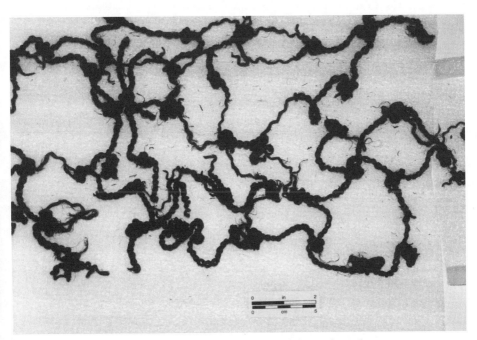

Fig. 3.7. Netting from Key Marco site. Collections of the Anthropology Division of the Florida Museum of Natural History. FLMNH Cat. No. 92-41-7.

and house poles, foreshaft of spear imperfect.[18] Worked til six. Home and after dinner sailed—a perfect moonlight night. Bed early.

Gause wrote in his diary, February 29:

Saturday morning went to work cove full of water & suggested making a gutter which was done. Gelousness [sic] followed by Mr. B- after that we got the water out and found several boles and pessels [sic] I found a net only one ever got Diner venison soup dined hearty . . . tonight boys all gone fishing Mr. & Mrs. Cushing gone sailing myselfe and Mr. Sawyer stays on board alls well now 9 o'clock Sat night going to bed . . . [Gause continued his diary for the next day.] Sunday morning got breakfast & went to Little Marco, myselfe Robt and Hutson got 4 ducks saw John Weeks come home Cushing well pleased with the delightful sports.[19]

Sunday 1st March, 1896

Up at half past six. Very well. Beautiful day. Sized as many as could of our beautiful specimens.[20] They are very difficult to preserve. Went down to excavatns just after dinner. Not very much water. Tried a place further east than any excv. but to near edge. Explored whole shell city site. It is precisely like key structures.[21] Discovered yet another water court which may prove of immense richness. Came home very tired. Slept little and awoke refreshed. After supper went for mail. Had letters from Mr. Safford & Mr. Cheyney containing frightfully domineering telegram from Doctor Pepper which cannot accept![22] Am awfully cut up about it. God grant wise decisions to me regarding it. Emalie worried too poor girl.

Monday 2nd March, 1896

Up at six after fearful night and with severe headache from worry. World all darkened again. Took on Calhoun this morning as agreed, and set men at work baling and clearing muck for further excavation.[23] Began finding superb remains at once—a net with gourd floats netted there to, float-block; spear butt, slats,[24] paddle shaped headpiece; line reel;[25] shell pick with perfect handle, drinking ladles (on in exploratn—cut had made down side of road ridge). Place unparalleled. Plummets of stone and shell; shell adze blade; scraping tablet of wood. Home still ill at 5pm. Better after supper and sat with Emalie on deck till could retire. Clear night and fresher. God grant rest at least.[26]

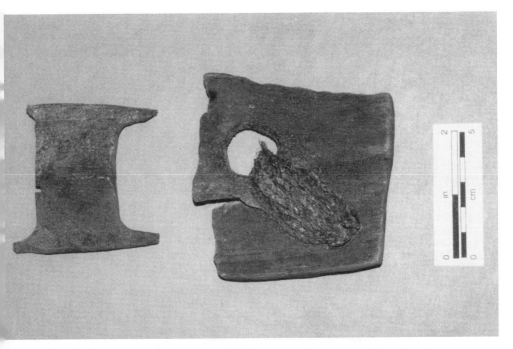

Fig. 3.8. Line reels from Key Marco collection. Collections of the Anthropology Division of the Florida Museum of Natural History. FLMNH Cat. Nos. A5691 and A5525.

On Monday, Gause wrote:

> Monday morn got to work found some very nice spicments [*sic*] such as pots bowls knives spears needles and carved wood along with a conno [canoe] spar 14 ft long which was very interesting to Mr C. . . . Tuesday morning all well but Alfred Hutson gone to work found everything lovely found some very fine speciments night a game of cards Then comes Mr. Barnes a deff and dumm man Frank's father but Frank could talk to him all OK got 2 opossums for 25 cts went to bed.[27]

Tuesday 3rd March 1896

> Up at six and breakfasted little after seven. Not very well but far better than yesterday and less depressed. Went to excavations soon after men and laid out their work. Baling and digging East Northwardly. Found stool, hitching block, harpoon points & prongs, needles, etc.[28] Returned soon and wrote on Dr. Pepper letter which finished afternoon made strong and

posted.[29] Wrote also to Major Powell and in evg, to Messers. Disston & Harden. Found sein[e] with pins; rope, adze handles, shell pick hafted; staff; little bowl; tablets of wood, bone, shell[30] matting[31] gourds,[32] canoe board, etc. etc. Marvelous results. Pd Barnes 1.00 and for possums 25 cts. I OKd hunt with Sawyer.[33]

Wednesday 4th March 1896

Awoke early and arose at half past six much better. Bright day. Breakfast half past seven, at diggings soon after eight. Arranging on way with Captn Cuthbert to allow our storage of specimens in his packing house.[34] Began finds at once but returned via store with Emalie. Letter from Dr. Pepper much more agreeable than telegram which answered so signally yesterday. Returning to diggings found Bergmann had discovered mask N.W. Coast in type painted black & white, followed soon by another, less perfect but handsomer.[35] Seine with shell sinkers attached. 100 pins of catfish spines; Spear prongs. Club with handle; pounders, superb wooden cups, magnificently carved bone; dirk, adze or chisel socket of bone with wooden handle; shell with bark wrapping for grasping, small dish of stamped black earthen, beads, pendants, bobbets of stone and shell.[36] Another mask and the most finely finished nest of 5 bowls and vase all wood ever yet found. Greatest day of my life in exploration.

In that final, climactic statement, Cushing ends this journal. It was written partially in sequence, then upside down and backward. Another journal must have begun the next day, March 5, 1896. Gause began to make noted reference in his diary to his role in the excavations, especially now realizing the monumental importance of the work he was doing and the discoveries of the expedition. George Gause wrote about March 4, and then the diary filled in where Cushing's diary ends:

Wednesday morning breakfast all well Mr. C had a bad headache but is better all goes to work the happies day ever gleaned on Marco Mr Burgman found 3 mask faces Robt 1 mall Alfred 5 bowls George Gause found 100 needles and 1 ball of wax then went with Mr C to examin some other places Home to supper Mrs. C over joyed with the curioes of the day Mr. Sawyer says he can't talk when he saw them beauties we have found Mr. Clark found a shell matted over nicely besides other thing too tedious to mention. . . . [Gause continued], March 5 Thursday morning Mr. Sawyer has finished servaying the Indian city at Marco, Mr. Cushing gives Gause full controll of the men to excavate the cove and mounds to the best of his ability and have his own way with the work . . .

On March 5, 1896, Maggie McIllvaine Collier, Captain Collier's wife, began her diary with mention of the Cushing excavations and finds. "Mr. Cushing and party are digging for curios . . ." She continued on March 6:

Mr. Cushing dug up a pr. of sun shills about four inches long, one side was painted in black on the inside, a man with fancy head & arm rig, & dug a turtle's head carved of wood, with a snout 2 in. long, it is hollow, it is painted in black and white, these are dug from below the muck which is 2 ft. deep, are bedded in marl, and must have been put there by these people before Columbus' time. When they find anything nice they all give a yell and Mr. Cushing shakes hands with the one who made the find. They are making a very thorough investigation, are wheeling the muck out on the shell hills where it will be convenient for us to get it for the field. This expedition is sent out by the University of P.A. and must cost a lot although the gentlemen of the party are volunteers.[37]

Although Mrs. Collier wrote Cushing found the controversial painted dancer shell, she most likely spoke in generalities of Cushing and his group. George Gause in his diary of March 5 and March 6 indicated who made the various finds; and his later statement of February 10, 1904, claims to have made the discovery of the painted shells himself.[38]

[March 5] Thursday doings went work early got some very interesting speciments 1 lyons image 1 turtle head all of good hard wood 6 bowls 2 pessels some carved boards 1 ball wax 2 little cannos 1 plumbett rapped with thread and waxed found by Robt Day went off nice bowls found by Alfred bowls and pessell by George Turtle George Lyon and woman found by Mr. Cushing. Mrs. Cushing seems well delighted. . . . [March 6] Friday the 6 went to work early soon found the most purfect painting ever found by an excibiter a pair of shells with Indian painted inside the I found a turtles head purfect then an Indian adz & 2 bowls 3 mallets 2 plumets 1 beautifull gorge found by Alfred Mr Clark found some nice thing such as pessell plummets an a head dress so we come in all well.

George Gause continued to record in his diary in his vernacular style the daily events. On March 7, Cushing wrote to Dr. Pepper about his "startling" discoveries. The original written rough draft text prior to corrections reads:

Yesterday my chief assistant (in digging) Mr. George Gause found under four [feet] peat a closed shell in which was a painting of a Dancer in all his paraphernalia represented! I found at the same time nearby a statuette of hard wood of the Mountain Lion God, equal in all ways to any from Egypt or Assyria. Yesterday painted masks were found by Mr. Bergmann and the timbers of fallen dwellings everywhere by all the men. Yesterday I made the crowning find an altar tablet of cypress wood bearing a distinct though faded painting of the King-Fisher-God bearing his double paddle as insignia, with word signs issuing from his mouth—precisely as in paintings of the Central American and higher Mexican codices.[39]

Cushing and his team had a surprise visit from Major Powell the second week of April. He was very impressed and pleased with the collections but bade the excavations to stop and to expedite packing the specimens.

Confirmation of Reef and Key Theories

With the Key Marco specimens packed, the successful Pepper-Hearst Expedition began preparation for its sail back to Tarpon Springs. Cushing desired more information concerning the key-dwelling prehistoric peoples. Their shell settlements fascinated him, and he endeavored to grasp as much additional information as he could while the means were still available to him. Always the anthropologist, Cushing surveyed the landscape of the mangrove islands he encountered, visualizing the habitation on the shell mounds that loom up from the topography. His earlier acquaintance with many of these sites led him to further explore the coastal surroundings with incredible energy.

The *Silver Spray* made several stops on her return trip. Demorey's Key, Weyson's Key, Battey's Landing, and Mullet Key were named in this Cushing diary as the entries now became sporadic. The description of Weyson's Key, a name now lost to history, with its "gigantic shell settlement," most likely fits Galt Island. On April 20, Cushing wrote to Dr. Pepper that the work was completed, specimens were aboard, and the schooner was under way to St. James City. He also mentioned the plan before final departure to photograph the great mounds at Battey's and the conch sea wall on Demorey's Key.[1]

Wells Sawyer's documents and George Gause's diary help fill in the missing days before the schooner reached the Anclote River.

Friday, 24th April 1896
    Not up until half past five but aw[a]ke sooner and had to pipe all hands on deck and call down Hudson and others sharply. Emalie not well dreadfully worrying, but she arranged to go over to the Whitesides later.[2] Left at seven. Before nine had purchased provisions, trowels and sickle for trip and off for Demery's.[3] Stopped on way at Weyson's Key a gigantic settlement

Fig. 4.1. Conch shell wall at Demorey's Key. Courtesy of American Philosophical Society.

with seven very high nearly parallel mounds & many lesser & with superb canal and water court or long bent lagune in middle.[4] Sawyer and I mapped roughly. Noon when had done. Excavations some promising (in muck). Crew hard to keep working. Came on to Demory's for dinner. As soon as over began cleaning Temple mound shell wall or Teocalli.[5] New out works developed. Staid to clean off for photographing and to plan by pacing. Survey will be nearly perfect. Looked great works over in moon-light. They are grand and beautiful. Will finish in morning and go back via Battie's by night.[6]

Wind died down made bed on strand. Sandflies little troublesome but not so much as expected. 11 oclock. God bless our work and aid & haste. Enlar[g]ed in other book.[7]

Fig. 4.2. Seminole bangles found at Fishermans Key. Collections of the Anthropology Division of the Florida Museum of Natural History. FLMNH Cat. No. A6812.

George Gause wrote in his vernacular style in his diary the following account:

> Wednesday Apr 22, 96 about 1 p.m. all well good for us all OK In the afternoon we excavate a mound at St James find a ketchin [midden] in wich we found a No of relax [relics] of all kinds . . . the 23 Thursday comes went south Key until 1 p.m. then to fishermans key by the sharpey to excavate a mound. . . . Friday morning we go to St James for Mail water tobacco fish tackel to go to Demerrys Key 10 miles NE we go to 3 other names we name Demerrys Key Josalyn Key Smith Key and Gauses Key named by Mr. Cushing we saw the great wall made by prehistorical indians the mounds are not by the thousands Thes mounds very high one 163 ft on which Gause is placed under 3 live oakes to measure the mound and a photograph taken of

him on the mound Gausie near the key we stayed ther till 10 at night on account of the tide then we camp again.

Saturday 25th April 1896
This page was dated but had no journal entry. Cushing skipped many pages and wrote from the back of the book to the front from this point. Cushing wrote another letter to Dr. Pepper, headed "Schooner 'Silver Spray' Caloosa Entrance, (St. James City,) S. Florida. 27th April 1896."

Your very pleasant letter of the 20th awaited my return from Demorys Key. It gives me new heart to know you have provided a place, temporarily at least, for the very fragile and precious portions of the collection from Marco. They will require almost immediate attention and many of the specimens will not bear the slightest handling by anyone until put together by myself, and then only by a personally trained assistant until finally treated and catalogued. . . . You have removed the greatest dread from my mind, and I thank you. The collection must I feel, be saved at any cost, for it is priceless, being unique in many ways.[8]

Cushing continued to thank Dr. Pepper for the offer to stay with him while he worked on the collection, but Mrs. Cushing and he must first visit with Mrs. Hearst in Washington to tell her of the finds.

The Gause journal continued:

Sunday comes we look at St James with wishfull eyes but to Fishermans Key to get the beads and corpse [sic] gun and other thing we can we sail down in the Spray nearby Sunday morning 26 went to get the corps we find 18 bullett 2 qts bealls 2 knives some sulphur 3 pipes we come home in a heavy blow to supper Mr. Cushing lost his watch in Charlota's Harbour all well at bedtime Apr 26.[9] Monday comes the 27th we stay on board and pk [pack] up the speciment until 4 oclock when a fearefull storm comes up and takes up the Silver Sprays anchor.

The following day, Gause called Tuesday 28th, he wrote:

. . . at daylight we hoist and set sail from Charlotte Harbour to Capt Teavy Pass [Captiva Pass] where we are to spend a night Turn turtle and get shells all are well and in good cheer . . . then to beach and a photo of a shell wall at Capt Teavy Pass and then a bath and set sail for Bogousage Light and egmount and for Anclote . . . we come to Anclote Wednesday morning we

Fig. 4.3. Cushing's sketch of shell structures at Shaw's Point. Brooklyn Museum, Culin Archival Collection. Cushing Collection [6.3.026]:A240.

work packing up our speciments and blankets to take our departure from Spray for home at Tarpon Springs.

Gause closed and signed off the journal "Geo W. Gause." There was confusion of dating at this point. Cushing had the *Silver Spray* arriving at Mullet Key on Wednesday the 29th.

The Cushing diary began again.

Wednesday 29th April 1896
    When I awoke this morning I decided as we had sighted Egmont light, to go in and examine that and mullet Keys.[10] Especially in hope of getting some GumoAlamo.[11] Neither key contained shell works sand & palmettos in very beautiful profusion. Heavy swells passing Erment [*sic*]. Anchored off Quarantine dock Mullet Key & went ashore.[12] Found no signs of primitive occupancy.[13] Sawyer Gause & the wakeful Dorsett fished. Bergman hunted

shells. Opp shores & northern may have camp sites—Began makes thro middle. Took bath at point, returned and as weather threatened determined to anchor for afternoon & night in mouth of Mullet Key & explore shell mounds reputed there. On arriving (not until 4) found on S.E. point great shell foundation comparable to any lower down. Sea washing away one end and had there perfect section from top of first terrace of platforms to water level. All stages of building recognized by Sawyer as well as self here.[14] Sawyer took section. Had Gause & Hudson dig to base twenty inches down to bar sand and oyster reef, all artificial as above. A complete confirmation of reef and Key theories. Explored peninsula with Bergmann. Chopped some bolls of Gumoalamo—here as elsewhere on keys prevailing. The platform mounds very high each with terraces & courts connected by graded way. Beyond, body of settlement succession of canals, levees and embankments—rectangularly laid out with numerous still slightly flooded water courts. Paced principal levees—one 154 yds & SW. with canal betw it & next six yards wide joined 59 yds. from rivershore by N. & S. Court 2 yds wide—one N. & S. Took points for sketch plan. Explored great burial mound back in pine sand land 1/4 mile—reached by two ridges or banks of canal—also cut off by sea—1/8th mile long cut midway betw settlement and tumulus. Nothing but outline sketch, as plates all gone save 2. From heights four other shell structures visible; but able by dark only to observe this—a great promise. Back at boat by eight. Bed at ten with orders for early start in morning. Tennison very indisposed.

Thursday 30th April 1896

Wakened by Emalie at half past 4. No one moving. Dressed enough to call up Captn Tony and crew and [No more written that day].

Friday 1st of May 1896

We sailed all night no available pass being reached and no dr[a]wning us in to anchor. At about 2 morning I awoke. We were off Hog Island.[15] I deeply regretted we could not put in and dig the burial mound, but Emalie and all the rest are worn with it all![16] Sighted soon after Anclote Light, and reached mouth of Anclote little after five dropping anchor.[17] Began getting material out & packing at once. Heat blazing and work wearily hard. Made however good progress. Mr. & Mrs. Safford & Mary, Mr. & Mrs. Clemson and little boy came out in launch.[18] Sent in sharpie boat Specs mail from Clydes Sml favrble.[19] Note from Dr. Pepper & alsnt [?] one from George. Fearfully wet and tire. Bed after talk early.

Saturday 2nd May 1896

Up a little late this morning feeling very miserably, but went at work before breakfast. Finished packing and entering specimens, had books & papers sewed in bundles (of canvas) for franking, and ship moved in to Anclote abreast Sponge Harbor. Here have continued work of packing until nearly ten o'clock tonight. Sent another sharpie load (specimens woods and tools) in to Tarpon Spg landing & wrote Mr. Safford letter. Gause & Dorsett (who were delinquent this morning) and Hudson going. Latter not back yet—tide probably bad—always is here. Hard days work, but tomorrow will finish. Bed 10:30. [cryptic message; see Appendix B]

Cushing headed the pages in the rest of the journal with day and date, from Sunday 3rd May 1896 to Tuesday May 12th, but did not write any more in the diary.

Cushing arrived back in Washington on May 13 and immediately wrote Dr. Pepper concerning the situation he encountered on his arrival. Someone had leaked information regarding the discoveries in an article to the press. This upset Cushing tremendously, and he did not understand how this happened, for Pepper and he had planned for the first news release to be in the "journal." Cushing implored Pepper to believe "I am and I have been, absolutely loyal to you," as he avoided all news agencies. Cushing also stated he had cautioned and "muzzled" Sawyer not to tell about the discoveries. Nor did he believe Major Powell would have given out any specific information—perhaps only generalities. Cushing added, "They are not all my friends there. There are among them those who certainly would have talked had they supposed it would annoy me or advantage themselves."[20]

Cushing was also very perturbed to learn that some of his important mail was intentionally held, such as the bill of lading, which caused him such aggravation in Tarpon Springs.

5

"Lost" Manuscript Found

When Cushing settled down in a cottage in Haven, Maine, to write the manuscript of his Florida explorations, he diligently prepared for the undertaking with maps, reference books, and knowledge won from his own firsthand experience of the Florida landscape. For years Cushing absorbed prodigiously information cultivated from numerous sources. The few short months he spent as a Cornell University geology student developed his awareness of geological formation and its effects on the ecology and geography of the land. Cushing's prolonged enlightenment by the Zuni Pueblo culture permeated all his understanding of the Florida investigations. Throughout his investigations one grand epic theory formulated in his mind—a great continental arc of culture extending from Florida up through the Gulf States into Mexico and the Yucatán.

Cushing voraciously consumed anthropological books, essays, and articles. His association and early contact with Lewis Henry Morgan influenced his thinking. Morgan was considered the American authority in the Victorian era on social development, with firsthand ethnographic studies of native peoples. His sociocultural theories on unilineal evolution and classifications followed society's cultural development from "primitive" to the pinnacle of progress in the late 1800s. For many decades Morgan's generalized system in *Ancient Society* was the only comprehensive summary and the accepted doctrine of social organization. In the spirit of the times, other contemporary theorists, Lubbock and Tylor, as well as Cushing, joined Morgan in taking for granted that what "was simplar [*sic*] must be older" (DuBois 1960:380–81). Cushing also incorporated the Morgan concepts and terminology in this manuscript, with terms such as "phratries," referring to related clans.

Although Franz Boas's anthropological thinking attempted to refute Morgan's model of cultural evolution, Cushing appreciated his holistic approach to culture, particularly as applied to regional problems, as in the Northwest Coast.

Cushing brought new light on the currently accepted concepts of totemism. He must have been aware of Emile Durkheim's theories on totemism that viewed totems as "the fundamental form of kinship division" . . . that composed . . . "the basic structure of society." Durkheim believed totemic beliefs gave "simple" societies their social and religious cohesion that contributed to "social solidarity" (McGee and Warms 1996:92). Cushing expanded totemic interpretation as not only social order, religion, or a pure art form, but also to include mundane utilitarian objects such as pottery and tools.

Cushing also drew from Edward B. Tylor's work *Researches into the Early History of Mankind* (1964) and *Primitive Culture* (1958). Cushing applied Tylor's concept of "survivals" archaeologically, again in a utilitarian form. Cushing discussed at length stages of "ears" on pottery that graduated to knobs. He described the stages of tool making in detail and contended that continuities in form carried forward into later stages, not always as Tylor implied by "force of habit" having lost the original function, but sometimes to "mature" a reproduced object. Maturation of a newly made object instilled powers that belonged to the older, very useful object. Often this took the form of a high polish on the new utensil or tool.

One of Cushing's major contributions to archaeology, experimental reproduction, won the admiration of his colleagues. Cushing fine-tuned this process through the years, culminating in the explanation of various concepts that he called "inferences."

The main portion of this elusive untitled manuscript resides at the National Anthropological Archives and was never published during Cushing's lifetime. No doubt, through the years, researchers glanced through the voluminous half-typed pages where Cushing often elaborately detailed seemingly minuscule encounters of geography and people and did not recognize it as the lost Florida manuscript. John Goggin did extensive research on Cushing in the late 1940s and referenced Cushing in his report *The Archeology of the Glades Region, Southern Florida,* (n.d.), but did not indicate knowledge of this manuscript.

Marion Gilliland intensively searched for the manuscript in the 1970s. She mentioned it in both of her books (1975, 1989) and again in a letter dated November 23, 1971, to Dr. William C. Sturtevant, curator of North American Anthropology at the National Museum of Natural History, Smithsonian. Gilliland wrote, "Maybe we will be fortunate enough to turn up some of those 'more than 1000 closely typed pages' Cushing referred to so often" (Gilliland research notes, Florida Museum of Natural History).

This chapter synthesizes the main portion of the manuscript, some 708 pages, now published as a companion volume, *The Lost Florida Manuscript of Frank Hamilton Cushing*. Cushing clearly organized the manuscript into parts that contained the principal aspects of his investigations that contributed to his evaluation and resulting "inferences." After Cushing's death, Major Powell attempted to salvage the writing and still have the manuscript published. Powell hired Wells M. Sawyer in 1901 to compile the manuscript (Sawyer 1901). Sawyer spent about sixty hours organizing the pages and noted associated plates in the margins to accompany the script. Powell died the following year before any further progress could be accomplished on the manuscript.

The first portion of the manuscript pertained to the geography of the west coast of Florida and Cushing's visual survey of the landscape. The well-documented freezing winter of 1895 fortuitously enabled Cushing a view of the topography that others who followed in his footsteps, such as C. B. Moore, did not have. Cushing mentions the denuded trees, even the gum alama, that he climbed for better views of the landscape. Cushing avoided the term *gumbo limbo,* which he considered a "corrupted" collo-quialism to describe the "ruddy trunks and limbs of these monstrous trees" he encountered. Very quickly Cushing surmised the gum alama was often associated with shell mound construction.

Cushing proposed that many of the islands, or "keys," of the southwest Gulf Coast were in fact "artificial," meaning that they had been intention-ally constructed by the key dwellers to support their "shell cities." Cush-ing systematically built his case to support his hypothesis. He detailed the extensive shell structures and canals he saw in the prehistoric settlements as directly influenced by the environment and the coastal conditions. Cushing wrote pages on the topography of Florida, beginning with the 28th parallel latitude southward through Tampa down beyond the Florida Keys. He described the interior coastlands as covered with tall yellowish pines. In low sandy areas beneath the pines, saw palmetto grew "luxuri-antly," while in the higher rolling areas vegetation was sparse grass. Cush-ing described the dune lands, lakes, marshes, and fen lands. The cypress swamps were of particular interest, most of a circular nature that would often have a raised area or hammock with tall pines rising above the cy-press. Cushing observed that these areas were composed of "shell and re-fused soil thereby marking some ancient Indian retreat or settlement."

Cushing described the chain of succession that formed these hammocks that eventually became Indian habitats, then rich gardens for the later settlers.

Cushing described the soil of southwest Florida in general terms as made up of sandy calcareous material mostly comprised of carbonate or sulfate of lime. Rain percolated through the sand into the limerock substratum, often dissolving it into a honeycombed formation leading to sinkholes that were sometimes basins and other times very deep holes.

Cushing's initial trip and investigations impressed upon him the ecological nature of the relationship between ancient cultures and environments. The remarkable shell mounds and structures began at the mouth of the Manatee River, southward from Tampa Bay to the southern tip of Florida. Mounds were concentrated in areas of estuaries, where numerous rivers, such as the Myakka, Peace, and Caloosahatchee flow into the narrow passes that lead to the Gulf waters. Canoe transportation was an efficient mode of travel, allowing for ancient settlements to develop for miles up the rivers. Outer series of islands formed parallel to the coastline, creating inland waterways. Cushing compared this topography to portions of the Bahamas, Antilles, and north and south coasts of Cuba, as well as the Yucatán and some Gulf Coast regions. Influenced by geological uniformitarianism, he wrote, "Like conditions will be found to have given rise to like phases of aboriginal development." Through extensive studies of comparative topography, Cushing perceived that the explorations of 1895–96 transformed from a local regional aboriginal development into a "very general subject of investigations."

Cushing, having laid the foundation of his theory and its widespread significance, began its confirmation in island and key descriptions. Cushing recognized that the stages of mound building followed a set pattern. The initial stage often began below the current waterline at low tide, sometimes eighteen inches to three feet. The base was always on an original coral or shell reef or oyster bar. Prehistoric builders formed a firm foundation on this base of large and medium interlocked conch shells. Sand quickly would shore up this area to elevate the construction. Other layers of shell in turn overlie these. Randolph Widmer's investigations of the Key Marco site (8Cr48) in 1995 described the shell construction he encountered. "This stratum was composed of multiple layers of *Busycon* shells tightly packed to form a level, prepared platform surface" (Widmer 1996).

Cushing stated that the shell constructions followed the natural distribution of the reef and generally followed a course parallel to the coast. He claimed some twenty-five of ninety keys stretching from Charlotte Harbor to Sanibel that disclosed some artificial construction. The ancient key builders continually added canals and watercourts to their domains. Fish preserves eventually became enclosed and turned into low-lying gardens. Other times these sites were abandoned and revealed only rudiments of initial-stage construction.

Casey (also Cashe's or Garden) Key, the most northern portion of "Barras Islands," located in Pine Island Sound, was one of these remarkable developments Cushing described in detail. This group of islands, located on an 1899 map prepared by the U.S. Army Corps of Engineers, is now known as Part Islands. After Cushing maneuvered through an "almost impenetrable jungle of mangroves," he emerged onto shell banks that rose to platforms that ascended to heights of extensive mounds that surrounded a lake or central lagoon. The three largest of these flat-topped mounds, whose summits reached twenty-five and thirty feet, were divided by graded ways that led to canals extending northwest and northeast. Other extensive mounds radiated easterly and southerly from the central watercourt, separated also by deep canal openings. These were difficult to explore because of the tangle of low dense vegetation and thorny vines. Apparently on one of the north platforms, Cushing evidenced the remains of a long-abandoned settler dwelling with a few sparse fruit trees. The entire complex was five-eighths mile long by three-eighths mile wide, and in several points was defined by steep embankments of shell walls. Tidal currents still flowed sluggishly from the deep northern channel to the wider southwesterly channel. Much of the lagoon was now filled with muck.

The great central lagoon margins on the north end consisted of large conch shells that appeared to have been arranged in an "orderly manner." Cushing observed hundreds of discarded shell tools, such as adzes, picks, hammers, and gouges. He considered Garden Key an exceptional example of an "ancient city," with all of the aspects of artificial construction.

Cushing's next stop was Useppa Island. Although he did not excavate in this initial reconnaissance of May 29, 1895, Cushing thought the island beautiful and the most picturesque of the keys. Many of his ideas developed there. As Cushing surveyed the landscape, he formulated the complete concept of the key dwellers' existence and their impact on the environment. Cushing described the topography of the island and speculated that the original inhabitants had abandoned artificial construction at an early stage, for the site was not developed extensively. He thought that the

clear pool of fresh water was chiefly a "rain reservoir" intentionally constructed to function as a cistern. He saw the remains of these basins in
other keys that he investigated. He described the rich vegetable gardens of
the Spanish tenants and the sherds of Spanish pottery tilled up to the surface.

Cushing walked inward on paths from the north end of the island as far
as the dense vegetation would allow. At a bluff he observed "pottery of the
ancient kind" and emerged at a spit where fishermen's huts were erected
on pile formations on the protected side over the water. A photograph of a
Spanish-Indian woman and child taken in 1895 must show the scene
Cushing encountered (Marquardt 1999:204; Pearse 1954). This scene occurred to him as a living image of the aboriginal fishing stations that perhaps once stood around the lagoons or watercourts.

Leaving the island in the shoal waters, Cushing observed the water
fowl: the stalking of the cranes, the communal fish drives of the cormo-
rants, and bands of diving pelicans. Here Cushing visualized the lessons
taught the ancient key dwellers by the "primeval fisherman of nature."

A picture formed in Cushing's mind about how the shell construction
got started. The earliest ancient reef dwellers built their huts on stilts such
as the Spanish fishermen's huts. Next, the stilts or piles were reinforced
with packed shells. Discarded food shells filled in the spaces or voids and
added to the stability of the foundation. These perhaps existed around the
margins of lagoons. Here canoes could pass through open ways at low tide,
driving fish inward, like the predatory water birds did. Over time, these
accumulating shells formed shell ridges, which were further added to by
sand and silt washed in by the tides.

Cushing next explored Josslyn's Key. What impressed him most as he
reached this shore and climbed a steep pathway up a shell mound was the
deep, nearly square basin that covered some 3/4 acre. Shell mounds surrounded this watercourt like the one at Garden Key, with graded ways and
deep canals that appeared to be long, straight, and continuous. Cushing
described the topography: "The higher mounds on this great Key were not
less than 27 or 28 feet above mean water level." Although the watercourt
had filled with muck, Cushing and his skipper managed to excavate a hole.
Here he found black potsherds, two or three plummets of shell, and a
Busycon shell tool with the remains of a broken wood handle. These finds
confirmed Cushing's ideas that these square or round watercourts that
seem to occur in all the shell settlements had once been "nearly sur-

rounded by platforms upon which stood the dwellings of the ancient inhabitants."

Cushing continued his reconnaissance of Josslyn's Key and described an amusing confrontation with a mother raccoon and her family, which led him to the western or storm side of the key, and remnants of an ancient sea wall. This, Cushing remarked, was "characteristic of all the greater keys." From here Cushing sailed in a sharpie, a small, masted boat, slowly through mud-shoaled waters toward Pine Island and Battey's Landing.

Barking dogs greeted the visitors, as did the forlorn tenant of this garden spot, who graciously guided Cushing on a tour of the place. Cushing described the site now known as Pineland in detail as he walked the terrain. Climbing to the summit of one of the great mounds, he was astonished by the extent of the ancient city. He followed the main canal for over a mile and observed "lesser canals running at right angles to the main one." Cushing later learned of other connected shell settlements, one across Pine Island at the edge of Matlacha Pass and another at the northern end of the island accessed through a branch canal.

Cushing also discovered a perfectly oval mound where wind had exposed human remains. By barely scratching the surface Cushing recovered the finest of thin potsherds of bright red earthenware with reticulated patterns.

His explorations continued all day, finding other canals and watercourts, now muck-filled, as well as flat-topped mounds. One of these cleared by fire showed its outline distinctly. The space was narrow, probably occupied by a public building, that too "must have stood upon posts or piles made fast, in the solid shell surface." All evidence firmly convinced Cushing that keys that now formed capes of the islands were first built keys (other than natural sandbars) and were the result of ancient engineering.

Each key and island that Cushing visited on his journey southward reconfirmed this concept. On Demorey's Key, Cushing described in detail his climb up a giant gum alama for a better vantage point only to fall with a rotten limb into a mass of vine that covered an amazing shell wall. Cushing arduously crossed the key, exploring all aspects of the ancient settlement, which he described in detail. He then excavated at several spots. Concrete-like marl encountered three feet below the surface in one excavation was, in Cushing's opinion, the foundation for the earliest development of the key.

Cushing surmised that Demorey's Key was completely built of deposits resulting from long continuous habitation. He also noted the historic occupation of the key. He supported his initial reconnaissance with further investigation in the expedition the following year.

This whirlwind trip then turned southward, after a short stop at Cayo Chino. Cushing described Ellis's Place on Sanibel Island in lengthy detail, identifying numerous sites that have yet to be recorded. An excavation in a shell ridge exposed a layer of thick marl embedded with fragments of pottery, shell, and bone. This stratum seemed to serve as support for posts or poles that had once been placed into the heavy shell foundation, now evidenced by several postholes. Further excavation revealed other post-holes at right angles, as though a corner of a structure. This most likely is the first identification of postholes in Florida archaeology.

Many settlers Cushing met remarked on Mound Key, "the highest mound in South Florida." As Cushing sailed among the mangrove keys, he could see this point rising above the rest.

C. B. Moore criticized Cushing's description of this key, but Wells Sawyer supported and substantiated Cushing's observations as well as his own. To this extent, when Sawyer organized the manuscript for Powell after Cushing's death, he added into the pages a map he drew and initialed from his own notes of 1896 from Mound Key. This map looks nothing like Moore's sketch of Mound Key (Mitchem 1999:185) but compares to Cushing's exceedingly detailed description. The photographed plates noted on the map could be further documentation.

The Johnsons, settlers on the island, showed Cushing their collection of ancient relics. These included Spanish medals and crosses of gold, silver, and bronze, and ear bangles of the later Seminole occupation. Mrs. Johnson told Cushing about another of their discoveries, a buried chamber, deep in one of the remote hammocks. Mr. Johnson had fallen into a chamber lined with charred wood as he probed a burial mound for more gold objects. In the chamber were found a "few objects of beaten gold," among the "human remains of the bone heaps." Her description of a depository of the dead reminded Cushing of the charnel houses of the Juan Ortiz account of Tampa Bay. Cushing's imagination took over. He could see the houses of the dead, raised on pilings in the center of small dug lakes, and he could see them being "periodically burned with their dismembered chests, or packet enclosed skeletor contex [sic], ere other structures were reared to serve, in turn, their period as receptacles of the dead."

Cushing pushed on to Key Marco with few stops on the way. At Naples he lamented not having enough time to investigate the deep aboriginal canal there, apparently dug to allow passage to an inner settlement. He finally reached Big Marco Pass and Collier's Island. The rainy season settled into the region and with it the famed Marco mosquito. Cushing was determined despite difficulties to fulfill his mission.

With hired help, Cushing excavated near Durnford's discoveries in the muck-filled watercourt. They banked the first eighteen to twenty inches of the black brown muck around a three- or four-foot-wide by five- or six-foot-wide excavation unit, in an attempt to keep out water. Cushing theorized that this muck-filled watercourt was like the numerous ones observed on his journey. These were not accidental deposits but would contain artifacts generally distributed throughout. Most of the objects came from a depth of less than three feet. Cushing encountered the remnants of building material, thatching, small timbers, and one large timber or spar. Two days of difficult excavation brought forth shell tools, earthenware cooking bowls, trays and vessels, a gourd cup, and abundant charcoal, indicating a domestic habitation. Cushing was satisfied that this ancient key characterized by and identified with structures he saw at other keys.

Upon returning to St. James City, Cushing discharged his crew and rested for a day. Obsessed now with proving his theory about the cultural origins of the keys, Cushing continued exploration of Pine Island and the surrounding keys. At St. James City he saw evidence of the early stages of key builder construction, perhaps stopped by some catastrophic storm. He observed strata in ridges on exposed slopes; one shell ridge resting on another separated by the black earth streak of habitation on the original surface.

Cushing and a Scotsman named Montgomery embarked in a dinghy to revisit the places he first observed. Convinced of the validity of his theory, he sought to reexamine the greater of the keys, perhaps to now "recognize many significant features" he might have "failed to see or understand."

At Battey's Landing (Pineland), Cushing excavated in the main canal and branch canals. He found traces of timbers in the canals at three to four feet deep. Cushing surmised that often canals were shored up with wood, and indicated a possible gate system at the intersections. He next excavated a trench in the north section at the top of one of the mounds. Here he observed distinct strata and loose pockets in the shell, which he interpreted as evidence of posts once supporting structures that "crowned" the mound.

Cushing then engaged Johnny Smith to help him with a few last days of exploration on the different keys. These investigations convinced Cushing that most all keys of artificial origin were constructed in various stages.

He found additional evidence of postholes on Sanibel Island. He devoted many pages of this manuscript to confirmation of his theory. Rains now changed his mind about one aspect. The small, deep, round basins he first judged to be small watercourts on low platforms must instead have been cisterns. Although perhaps once filled with fresh drinking water, the water now was often salty because of high tide and sea level rise.

After six arduous weeks of exploration, Cushing rested at Captain Whiteside's to recuperate for the journey home. Whiteside asked Cushing to lecture at his store to the settlers of the area. Cushing was impressed with the wide geographical range of the intelligent guests who gathered in the smoke-filled room around the smudge pots to hear him speak of the Zuni days of his youth and his recent explorations. Cushing took full advantage of this evening, for after his talk, he asked questions concerning ancient remains in the interior of Florida. These hardy pioneers gave Cushing details of the inland works. Most were made of sand in a marsh environment, close to river sources and tributaries or connected to the great Lake Okeechobee by canals. Moats or lakes surrounded the built mounds described, and even the most remote usually contained seashells. Settlers mentioned finds of glass beads. This indicated to Cushing Spanish contact, and he surmised these sites must be the last traces of the ancient people. This description of an inland phase of key dweller culture convinced Cushing of the general archaeological significance of the key dwellers and their apparent influence on the Mound Builders phase of culture in North Florida and throughout the Southeast, but also into the Mississippi Valley.

On Cushing's return home, he twice was provided with opportunities to discuss the existence elsewhere of shell banks and mounds, first with an old Spaniard and then a Bahamian. Cushing was told indeed that the keys northward of Cuba and northwestward to "Utican" (Yucatán), as well as the Bahamas, had all these features of ancient works. This information expanded Cushing's first hypothesis to consider the sea currents of the Caribbean and Atlantic sweeping northward from the coast of South America through the numerous islands toward the Gulf Coast shores of Florida.

The origin of the so-called mound builders, although well investigated, continued to perplex the ethnologists of the Victorian era. An excited Cushing realized he now had a "working hypothesis" that involved "great archeo-ethnological problems." Cushing seized every opportunity the following year with the Pepper-Hearst Expedition to further develop the hypothesis and to support it from archaeological evidence.

To pass the time while awaiting the arrival of his schooner at Tarpon Springs, Cushing undertook an extensive investigation of the Safford Mound (8PI3). Ripley Bullen and colleagues' report (1970) on the Safford burial mound considered the extremely limited data then available on the excavation. The Florida manuscript and the Florida diaries add significant information to that report. The mid-portion of the manuscript character- izes the deposition of the burials in the mound and related funereal objects.

Cushing's research goal was to determine whether the construction of the mound was similar to the burial mounds he observed in Southwest Florida. After excavation reached a depth of three and four feet, Cushing wrote that "the mound had originally been built precisely as the ancient bone heaps [he] had explored at Ellis Bay and Mound Key; that is to say in the middle of a pond-like basin, this one, at least having been artificial."

A central deep transverse trench exposed the important feature of the mound; it was composed of three distinct strata. These building stages of the mound "represented widely separated periods of internments." Cush- ing detailed this cross-section of the mound with measured depths. The depth at the center of the basin was nine feet, six inches. The lowest stra- tum of burials measured three feet, seven or eight inches thick; the middle stratum barely three feet; and the top stratum of equal depth. Cushing surmised that because there were exposed remains on the surface, the sur- face stratum must have originally been at a greater depth.

The top level of burials was greatly disturbed by pothunters, and a trench was still evident from Walker's limited investigation in 1879. The middle stratum of burials was undisturbed previously, and the excavators left the interments in situ for Cushing's evaluations. Many of the burials were completely dismembered in a secondary bundle burial style and ar- ranged in a type of skeletal pack with long bones underneath, then smaller bones, then the skull placed on top. Matching potsherds on and around these interments indicated that whole vessels had been inverted over the packs or broken as a general sacrifice with the depositions.

Determined to further research the concept of stratified burials, Cush- ing decided to send his Smithsonian team some miles north to another mound site, Hope Mound (8PA4/8PA12), for investigation (Smith 1971). This preliminary research question was "speedily" confirmed.

The Safford Mound continued to yield significant information. Mul- tiple burials were encountered in the central portion of the mound. An important aspect of the mound was not only the diversity of modes of interment, but also the variety of what were described as sacrificial objects.

Most burials were interred with associated funerary objects from superb chipped stone "daggers," finely incised and decorated pottery, and stone, quartz crystal, copper, and shell plummets of sacrificial nature.

According to Cushing, there were three major modes of burial. These were dismembered bunched burials, "trussed up" burials resembling Peruvian mummies, and "pack burials," each containing an extended skeleton. All gave evidence of long preparation prior to some grand periodic burial. The pack burials, according to Cushing, appeared as though wrapped in "robes of fur or matting" or "thin slats of wood or baskets." These were usually associated with personal belongings. Distinguishable traces of fire remained on the surface of the burials, as though extinguished after lighting. There were few elaborate burials, only three or four, among the some six hundred individuals interred in the mound.

Three other minor modes of burial were evidenced. One represented death by violence. Another type indicated "cist-like" burials, where the skeletal remains were evidently on an enclosed construction, then, as with a pyre, fired and allowed to be only partially consumed. Burnt pine-knot stakes still remained and were collected by Cushing. The last mode consisted of infant burials in large conch shell ladles.

Cushing's sociological conclusions concerning the burials and the sacrifices formed from his prior connection with the Zuni and his knowledge of their "known notions" of tribal affiliations. Clan persons were buried with their clan group, each representing a totem. The totemic chiefs or elders were buried in their entirety with the most elaborate of rites. Red dry powder traces over the interments at the mound, and associated objects, helped to confirm this inference.

Groups of sacrifices located in each of the four quarters (north, south, east, and west) and one near the center of the mound further convinced Cushing that this was a tribal cemetery. The different quarters maintained the different totemic divisions of the tribe. Within each of these quarters the variety of burials occurred as though socially ranked.

Cushing surmised that the relationship of the burials with one another in each grouping also implied the social structure of these ancient peoples. The distinction between the classes of burials obviously conformed to a fixed system. This Cushing compared to the Zuni organization of mythic concepts and pointed to the stage in cultural development achieved by these prehistoric people. He then inserted into the manuscript pages portions of a previous report he had published, "Outlines of Zuni Creation Myths" (1896f), which explained the essence of the four quarters of the world and the central middle, or navel. Each quarter represented related clans identified by totems, such as animals, plants, or elements that bore an intimate relationship to one another. Cushing explained and gave examples, such as the Zuni clan of the north that are grouped "the Crane, the Grouse, and Evergreen." They are related because of their fitness for the region of the north, the cold, and the winter.

The quarters were further designated by color and associated natural factors. These clans are kinship groups with a female line of inheritance. The clans are often in natural groups of threes related by their particular fitness to the quarter, such as sun, sky, and eagle. The Zuni divide this arrangement even further, into a "6 or 7 fold arrangement," with upper and lower worlds, and the central world, or navel. This is the central arrangement that organizes their government, social, and ceremonial life.

Cushing used the Zuni "scheme of organization" to substantiate his archaeological theories about the Gulf coast. The sacrifices and groups of burials convinced Cushing of this designated system in the Safford Mound. Therefore, each of the four quarters was a tribal division and held a phratral burial group or a unilineal descent group of related clans.

Sacrifices in the four quarters of the mound consisted of groups of whole vessels with the bottoms punctured out or "killed." The fifth, or central, sacrifice contained pendants of extraordinary workmanship. One pendant was of finely shaped massive copper and another of rock crystal, an example of refined lapidary art. Rare minerals of mica, a stone of galena, and a pendant of gray diorite completed the composition of this sacrifice.

According to Cushing, ranking of individuals apparent in the burials was also evidenced by another attribute. Cushing observed the defined lines of cauterization to alter and scar the scalp and divest it of hair in a few of the skulls that exhibited "crest-like ridges." See Cushing (1897c:17–18). This cauterization or cicatrization of the scalp of a few individuals indicated a rank either totemic or achieved.

Specimens of designed pottery also confirmed this conception of totemic relationship. Cushing concluded the ancient peoples of the mound were less developed than the Zuni and had not attained their level of social organization.

The last hypothetical concept proposed in this manuscript primarily dealt with the origin of decoration. The Cushing concept of decoration was not as an art form, but as a transfer of utility and power to the object reproduced. Cushing perceived that the best of the art of prehistoric people—basketry, textiles, and especially woodwork—had totally disappeared in the sandy soil of the Safford Mound; only a few traces remained. Although Cushing described the recovered cultural remains of stone, shell, and bone, the ceramic objects exhibited the greatest variety of form and detail. Cushing based his description of pottery collection on decorated treatment, as most all vessels were of the coil process.

To begin, Cushing described the different methods of decoration, often a combination of stamping, paddling, and incising. Paddles of wood in carved and concentric design accomplished the stamping and paddling. These Cushing thought to have been of Caribbean type and were used to impress in series, so that it appeared as though a single stamp. Some of the finer specimens had a thin slip of differing color of paste from the temper of "exceedingly fine sand or pulverized pot-sherds." Incising was accomplished with pointed implements or bodkins, such as fingernails, columellae and edges of shells, small bird bones, and even reeds.

Ornamentation served several utilitarian purposes. First, properties and shape of the original utensil, such as a gourd or shell ladle, were used to transfer to the pottery the function of the original form as a continuation of its usefulness. This was perpetuation of apparent decoration in one type of material transferred to other materials. Cushing thought the early beginnings of pottery design signified the effort of the potters to recreate the wood ware the pottery replaced. Cushing conjectured that the origin of the stamped reticulated pattern was the graining in wood. Sometimes rollers of wood or a rocking tool were used to produce the pattern. Cushing admitted that this stamped pattern was very common in Florida and resembled basketry, but his experimental process showed that the cross-grained wood succeeded in reproducing this type of decoration.

Second, tattooed designs on the surface of the vessels invested the pottery or transferred the totemic of the tattooed pottery maker to the pottery. Cushing mentioned historic paintings depicting Native Floridians heavily tattooed. He specifically described two vessels with obvious totemic designs. One was a horseshoe crab depiction, and the other was a symbol of the "navel mark" used by the Japanese, Chinese, and Koreans. Cushing had no doubt the design of this symbol (today called yin-yang) was from a seashell cup where the whorl terminated. Cushing inferred this was another mode of investure or the transference of function from one object to another, "the common function of two different forms." This was a borrowed Zuni concept, founded on the premise that all living creatures have special forms for their existence and these forms characterize different actions and different functions. Maskoid designs were also included in this category. Several of the pottery vessels depicted masklike designs. One design Cushing called fish mask from the moment he looked at this vessel. It was an entire symbolic scheme of three panels representing different articulated fish, a fisherman, and pierced fish. Cushing felt this vessel may have been the maker's totem or that perhaps it was the maker's chief avocation. Other elaborate vessels had decorative complicated treatment of superimposed dual masks. Cushing compared this to elaborate Antillean and South American pottery.

The last concept in this theory explained the finishing of useful objects, not for the sake of ornamentation, but for practicality. Implements evolved from sticks, stones, shells, and bones. They were picked up and used simply for a certain purpose and kept for their usefulness. When they wore out, new implements were made to take the place of the old ones. The effort needed to reproduce a tool like the old one included copying all the characteristics and the appearance of the well-worn tool, even to the polish that developed on the tool from handling.

The old implements gained experience; they matured. So the toolmaker must reproduce not just a similar new object, but one matured and useful. Polish was the one indication of maturation. An unconscious effort to recreate the main characteristics of the older tool often reproduced nonessential features. The functional process of maturation and surface polishing developed from this simple concept to more elaborate mythic reasoning. Cushing again relied on his Zuni reasoning. Creatures and things in the world had two special phenomena. First, all had differing forms that differed by action. Second, all animate and inanimate forms change through maturity, even the immovable things such as rocks and bluffs. Accordingly, life attributes were given to things made and used, because life is strictly conditioned by form. Specialized form gives not only power, but also limitations. Utilitarian art form reflects this theory.

"Primitive" people sought to perpetuate the unknown powers or functions to the minutest detail in this reproduction of the earlier form. As arts became more highly developed, the artisan sought to multiply those powers. One method used to empower the object was toward animistic attribution of precise detail. As an example, a harpoon might be likened to a long-beaked bird of prey to convey the power of the bird to the recreated object. The same theory relates to the interpretation of wearing animal masks or tattoos to resemble by markings. So the craftsman added animal powers to the surface treatment, and a high complexity of art arose. This was demonstrated not only in weapons, but in utensils, where the tendency was to invest all sorts of things with desirable functions.

This complexity escalated; composite patterns were superimposed, and diverse beings combined. Symbols of totemic relationships were over-masked with personalities of other beings that they may be related to by birth or derived from, so as to multiply their beneficial influences.

The increasing elaboration gave rise to complicated and combined forms. In some cultures this culminated in writing. Cushing details this entire scenario as it progressed to a conventionalized form. The more highly developed the system became, the more obscure its origin.

Cushing's final synopsis equated these progressive stages of development that resulted in "calendric" representation. Here again, Cushing demonstrated clearly his conformance to Lewis Henry Morgan's concept of social development and nineteenth-century social philosophy. Writing, according to Cushing, had always begun as a priestly rite to record calendric or cosmical ceremonials and rituals. He thought the archaeological evidence of pottery from the Safford Mound showed a progression from the simple process of reproducing a pottery form to the elaborate ceramic cosmic designs of some of the Safford Mound vessels.

Cushing was correct about the long span of prehistoric history revealed in the Safford Mound ceramic record. Ripley P. Bullen's research (Bullen, Harris, and Partridge 1970) on the Safford Mound ceramics recognizes pottery types that span 2,000 years. Modern research, however, proved Cushing's developmental sequence wrong. The earliest pottery, Deptford and then Swift Creek (500 B.C. to A.D. 200), interred in the mound Cushing correctly identified. The most elaborate vessels, though, date to the later Weeden Island ceramic complex (A.D. 200 to A.D. 1000). Cushing, through lack of previous data, did not recognize the temporal placement of the less elaborate but distinctive Safety Harbor ceramics that developed in the last period of the mound construction. Continued use of mounds or reuse was commonly practiced in the central Gulf Coast region during the time span (Milanich 1994:227). Cushing noted there was no evidence of European contact in the mound site.

Cushing's ideas of cultural development are clearly the doctrine of the Victorian era. His use, though, of cross-cultural comparisons and experimental reproductions was innovative and beyond his contemporaries' thinking and time period.

6

Conclusion

Both the Florida journals and the untitled Florida manuscript contribute significant new information concerning Frank Hamilton Cushing and his archaeological investigations during 1895–96. Cushing has been characterized for too long as a "flash of brilliance" with little depth (Hinsley 1981: 205). Cushing acknowledged that although several others had greater archaeological ability, he confidently felt that he alone possessed the combined essential ethnographic background and archaeological skills that gave him insight to look beyond material remains to larger theoretical concepts. His Zuni experience taught him the "interrelation of things and how to interpret them" (letter to Dr. Pepper dated September 7, 1896 [Cushing 1896b]).

So what has been learned from the "school of Cushing"? One line of evidence comes from his fieldnotes. References to his notes appear several times in the manuscript and in the journals. Apparently, the fieldnotes were periodically brought "up to date" when he had a leisure moment. Cushing's background of the Zuni years trained him to keep extensive fieldnotes (Green 1979, 1990). There is no reason to assume he would have done otherwise in the Florida fieldwork years later. This is in contrast to the remarks of later writers concerning the failures of Cushing's field methods (Sanjek 1990:189–92). His detailed topographical observations, accounting for some three hundred manuscript pages, most likely were first written down in note form. His daily journal, written at night, summarized as a "running log" the events of the day. He recorded the weather, his physical condition, the letters he wrote, the day's events, and his delights and frustrations. He wrote page after page of correspondence, as noted in his journals. Many Cushing letters are collected in various institutions throughout the United States. We can only hope that one day the fieldnotes will also surface, as well as the other missing journals.

A crucial element of Cushing's initial exploration in spring 1895 was the hard freeze of that winter that dipped down into southwest Florida. The defoliation of the subtropical trees and bushes allowed Cushing an unobstructed view of the landscape. In his initial journey of almost eight weeks, as he contemplated the landscape Cushing quickly grasped the true cultural significance of the keys and islands. In this sense, the muck pond on Key Marco with its superb artifacts played only a peripheral role. By the time Cushing reached Marco he could identify the settlement patterns, so he hastened back to revisit all the islands and keys with renewed understanding, to make certain he did not overlook anything.

Cushing was a pioneer in innovative archaeological techniques. He formulated research questions prior to actual excavation. The Safford Mound was excavated initially to learn whether this site compared to the burial mounds near Ellis's Place on Sanibel Island and Mound Key. Cushing searched for connecting factors between and among regional peoples and cultures. The Hope Mound was excavated to support the findings of burial stratification observed in the nearby Safford Mound.

Cushing's experimental archaeological process, testing and retesting methods of reproduction to understand the working manufacture of implements, won the admiration of many of his colleagues. He used his ethnographic resources to gain knowledge of prehistoric lifeways. Cushing even used the term "great archaeo-enthnographic problems" that involved his research. This research went far beyond simple analogies of a direct historic approach and extended into the psyche of the aboriginal mind. Cushing detailed the thought processes of the toolmaker making an implement, and the potter coiling a pot. He gave numerous examples and the basis of reasoning that explained the concept of form and function. Without mentioning Cushing, Trigger's recent authoritative study acknowledged the value of his basic approach: "No one has ever considered replicative experiments as other than archaeological. Although strictly speaking they do not study material from the past, their relevance for archaeological interpretation, and for it alone, is unquestioned. On the other hand, while archaeologists have long relied on ethnographic analogies to interpret archaeological data, only recently has the carrying out of major projects of ethnoarchaeological research in an effort to learn more about the relations between material culture and human behavior been regarded as integral to archaeology" (Trigger 1989:371).

For three summers one of us (PK) excavated and mapped shell mounds in southwest Florida and can visually relate to Cushing's description and recognition of postmolds. Several excavations gave substantiation to his pile-dweller concepts. He understood the how and why of the foundation and how shell mounds build up over time. He recognized the strata of shell layering, and postulated how many of the keys were artificially built. Recent research substantiates his observations (Upchurch, Jewell, and De-Haven 1992:59–71; Widmer 1996, 1998).

Cushing used sieves in his investigations of the Safford Mound and the Key Marco site. When he realized that sherds from the Safford Mound might be crossmended to reconstruct vessels, he instructed workmen to preserve every sherd and directed that "the sand should be sifted in this effort and in the search for smaller objects, such as beads and other delicate ornaments." At Marco he also purchased a sieve, as noted in his journal entry of February 27, 1896.

Cushing believed in an interdisciplinary approach. Geology of the land guided the adaptation of the ancient peoples. He described the rise in sea level and its effects, and the formation of the land. Ancient cultures were part of the coastal ecology. Human action and natural process worked together to influence island formation in the specialized maritime ecological niche of southwest Florida.

Cushing was interested in archaeobotanical remains and recovered two types of gourds from the Key Marco site. These gourds were used as net floats (Cutler 1975:255–56). Cushing was convinced that small watercourts of the ancient key dwellers filled in over time and became vegetable gardens. On Casey, also referred to as Cashe's or Garden Key, his first stop on his initial reconnaissance, Cushing observed "gigantic clams" that appeared to have been used as hoes. He looked to linguistics to further demonstrate cultural connections: "the same word in Carib and Timucua signifies not only 'Fish-pond' but also 'Vegetable garden'" (Cushing 1897b). He also noted that a few of the blackened earthenware cooking bowls found at Key Marco contained charred remains of foods, "vegetable and fruit." Recent research of archaeobotanical remains on Pine Island gives evidence of plants that may have been associated with "neotropical homegardens" (Marquardt and Walker 2001:52).

Extraordinary information about sites in central and southwest coastal Florida is revealed in the journals and manuscript. Several sites, such as the Barras Islands, are unrecorded and undocumented. Cushing's observations and maps about many sites will add significant information and help guide modern researchers.

The aboriginal canal system in Florida has always intrigued archaeologists. Cushing mentioned and mapped many canals not identified today that need to be verified and documented. His investigations of wood supports used on some canal intersections and "branch canals" help support recent archaeological research (Luer and Wheeler 1997).

Cushing lamented the lack of basketry, textiles, and wood from the Safford and Hope Mound sites, writing in his manuscript that the "best of the art of such peoples has in nearly all cases totally disappeared." Even though he stated publicly the finds at Key Marco were "unusual," and most likely not replicated, he confided in letters to Pepper that only he and Sawyer (whom he explicitly trusted) knew of other similar wetland sites. He did not want to divulge locations because no doubt others would quickly follow to find and try to replicate his success at Key Marco, thus destroying future opportunity for scientific investigation (letters to Dr. Pepper dated March 7 and April 2, 1896, Hodge-Cushing Collection; letter dated August 2, 1896 [Cushing 1896b]).

The annotated journals present a mature Cushing, a man in his prime, confident of his abilities, yet still trying to prove himself to his contemporary academic community. He remained determined to be successful and with great effort overcame numerous obstacles throughout the expedition: lack of finances, poor health, flawed communication, sabotaged correspondence, and unscheduled delays. Cushing never lost sight of the magnitude of his explorations and worked ceaselessly to preserve, protect, and report his finds. In the end, he succumbed to pressure and illness, and eventually to an early death, and failed to produce the important monograph. The untitled manuscript, segmented and unfinished, languished unnoticed for one hundred years. With its publication, perhaps Cushing will become properly recognized for his contributions as a Florida archaeologist.

Appendix A

Silver Spray

The vessel *Silver Spray* played an important role in the success of the Pepper-Hearst Expedition. When Cushing arrived in Tarpon Springs to discover the *Silver Spray* was not in port, John Cheyney, one of the agents for the Disston group, tried to persuade Cushing to use a lesser boat, a sloop called the *Moccasin*. Cushing remained adamant that the *Silver Spray* was the vessel that would fulfill his needs. This decision set Cushing's mission back some ten weeks and resulted in several important outcomes.

First, an archaeological reconnaissance was conducted in this central coastal area that has never been duplicated, including the excavation of two important mound sites that gives the only comprehensive detailed information about the prehistory of the native peoples of this area.

Second, the decision provoked Cushing's problems, financial and health, and reveals the strength of Cushing's true character, to persevere under extraordinary pressures. This man was not a whiner of the Bureau of Ethnology as portrayed in later writings.

What became of the *Silver Spray* after its momentous voyage into history? The record of the vessel began with its construction at Sponge Harbor at the mouth of the Anclote River. According to the 1896 Merchant Book of the National Vessel Documentation Center of the United States Department of Transportation, the vessel was built in 1894 of wood, and rigged as a schooner, official number 116648. The registered dimensions were 52 feet long, 16.2 feet width, and 3.3 feet deep. Gross weight was 21.90 tons, and net weight 20.81 tons.

Wells M. Sawyer, in a detailed letter home from the "Marco Ship Channel," described and sketched the *Silver Spray* and auxiliary boats used on March 29, 1896. The vessel "is a 21.87 ton schooner carrying six sails." (See Gilliland Collection, P. K. Yonge Library, University of Florida.) He wrote that an awning had been rigged up over the cabin and quarterdecks for protection, and he counted fourteen persons living aboard the *Spray*.

Cushing on the sail to Marco called the *Silver Spray* a "beautifully sailing boat." For years after the expedition it sailed regularly between Key West and Tarpon Springs as a sponging vessel. The large schooner would serve as the mother ship, with long stays in the Gulf with small hook boats or, in later years, diving boats, retrieving the sponges. The *Florida West Coast Truth* records a sponge haul July 20, 1898, of 146 bunches of sponges.

Robert H. Pent (1964) describes his first sea venture on "this noble looking vessel" as a cook's helper in the early 1900s. John Cheyney then owned the vessel, and its skipper was Captain John Brady. Pent relates nostalgic stories of seas and the sturdiness of the "Queen" vessel.

The National Vessel Documentation Center registry lists six entries for the *Silver Spray* registered from 1894 to 1928. The last entry reads, "Abandoned June 30, 1928." This last entry finalizes the information available on the *Silver Spray*, a sad demise of a great schooner that left a brief mark in history.

Appendix B

Cryptic Messages

Hopefully, someone with linguistic or cryptic deciphering knowledge will undertake the task of interpreting Cushing's cryptic messages. Six times in the journal entries, Cushing wrote a cryptic line of symbols. The reason why he felt compelled to include these lines in his personal diaries remains perplexing. Perhaps he realized from his Southwest years that others would eventually read all that he composed. Were these messages a reminder to himself, or a source of strength and encouragement? The context of Cushing's problems must be considered. By the end of January 1896, he was under financial and emotional stress, not having heard from Dr. Pepper concerning his repeated requests for additional funds, and not able to dislodge the *Silver Spray* and proceed with his mission.

After many hours of study and comparison to foreign languages, antique shorthand books became available to one of the authors at an estate sale. Perhaps these are the key to decipher Cushing's personal thoughts. Benn Pitman wrote the first book in 1860, *The Manual of Phonography, The American System of Shorthand*. Benn Pitman and Jerome B. Howard reissued the book several times, in 1887, 1897, and 1903. The most helpful book acquired was titled *Palmer's Expert Reporter*, written by E. M. Palmer. It was first issued in 1890. This is a system of phraseology that begins with the study of phonography and combines symbols into usable phrases. Unfortunately, another book, *Palmer's New Manual*, was meant to accompany and guide the student initially in this system. That book was not available.

It seems apparent that Cushing used some form of shorthand to write the messages. He often would leave out vowels, as evidenced by his text in the journals. Although several elements of Palmer's phraseology are included in Cushing's messages, it appears Cushing individualized his shorthand. All the cryptic messages are included by date for comparison.

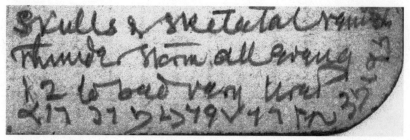

Fig. B.1. Cryptic message, January 22, 1896. National Anthropological Archives, Smithsonian Institution (MS 97-28).

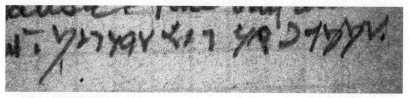

Fig. B.2. Cryptic message, January 24, 1896. National Anthropological Archives, Smithsonian Institution (MS 97-28).

Fig. B.3. Cryptic message, January 25, 1896. National Anthropological Archives, Smithsonian Institution (MS 97-28).

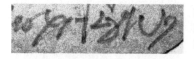

Fig. B.4. Cryptic message, January 26, 1896. National Anthropological Archives, Smithsonian Institution (MS 97-28).

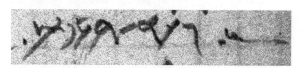

Fig. B.5. Cryptic message, January 27, 1896. National Anthropological Archives, Smithsonian Institution (MS 97-28).

Fig. B.6. Cryptic message, May 2, 1896. National Anthropological Archives, Smithsonian Institution (MS 97-28).

Appendix C

Comparative Studies

The following series of plates and comparative studies were intended by Cushing to illustrate his conclusions and accompany preliminary essays of the final and more general Report to the Bureau of American Ethnology on the Collections and Explorations of the Pepper-Hearst Expedition. These draft essays dealt with comparison of similar objects from widespread Native peoples that show like series of art forms that Cushing felt grew from weapons of war and evolved into protective rites of peace. Cushing explicated his reasoning and provided illustrations to demonstrate connections between the original Key Marco specimens and persistence of trends throughout time and space. In an essay titled "Key Marco Types," he wrote concerning tablet-amulets, "Hence and from the relatively large number of the original Marco specimens I reflected that this type of thing must have possessed paramount importance since it had persisted not only throughout the centuries separating the true Key Dwellers from their more inland representatives or successors and those from early historic tribes, but has held its own as well in three successively used materials, wood, stone, and metal."

The comparative series, plates 1–8, illustrate the duck amulet. Cushing elaborates in his first essay on the significance of the "duck as used in effigy by so many North American tribes." Cushing used the Zuni concept of the ever vigilant duck, "safest guide in the pathway of war, surest guard in the pauses of peace." (See Cushing, Key Marco Types, 1844-a, National Anthropological Archives, Smithsonian Institution.) Other comparative figures compiled by Cushing were to be used in various draft essays. In 1898, Cushing finished portions of the essay "Tomahawk and Calumet, Shield and Gorget" in time for competition, upon which he took honorable mention.

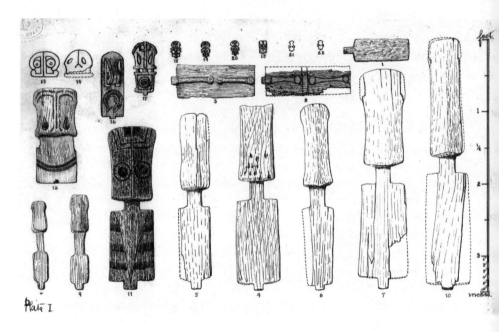

Fig. C.1. Plate 1, wooden tenon tablets to scale. By permission of Haffenreffer Museum of Anthropology.

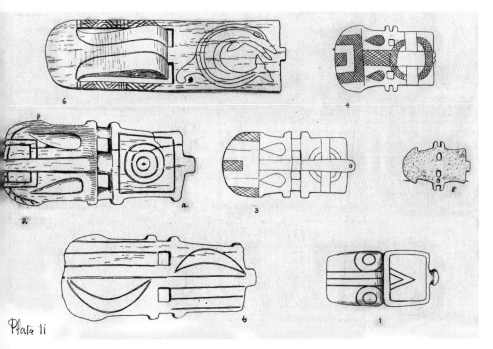

Fig. C.2. Plate 2, decorated wooden tablets or amulets. By permission of Haffenreffer Museum of Anthropology.

Fig. C.3. Plate 3, duck study. By permission of Haffenreffer Museum of Anthropology.

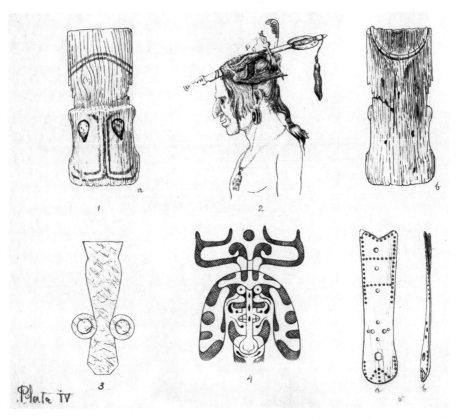

Fig. C.4. Plate 4, comparative headdress study. By permission of Haffenreffer Museum of Anthropology.

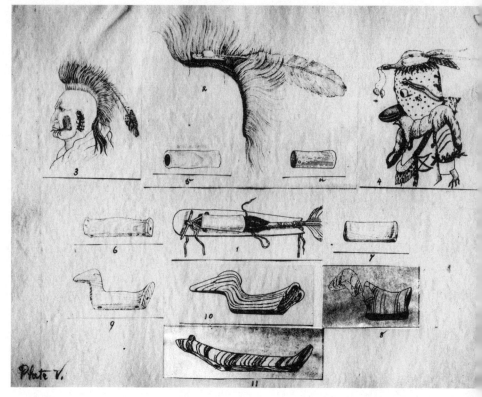

Fig. C.5. Plate 5, components of a headdress. By permission of Haffenreffer Museum of Anthropology.

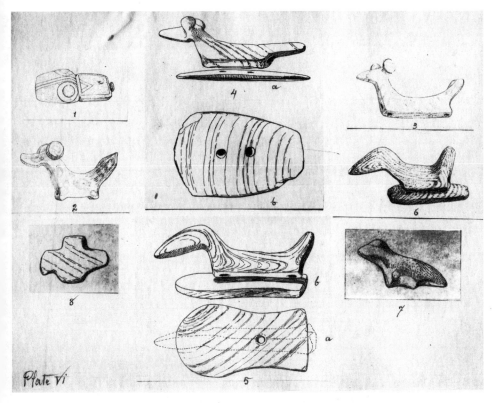

Fig. C.6. Plate 6, construction of an ornament study. By permission of Haffenreffer Museum of Anthropology.

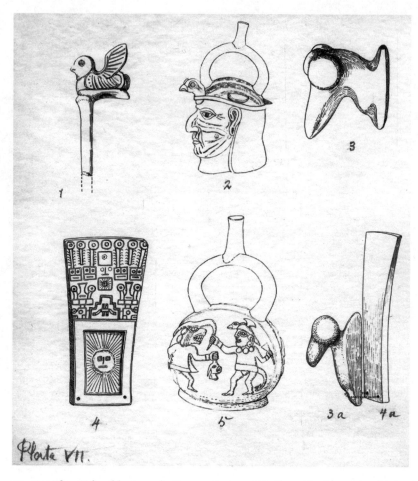

Fig. C.7. Plate 7, headdress study. By permission of Haffenreffer Museum of Anthropology.

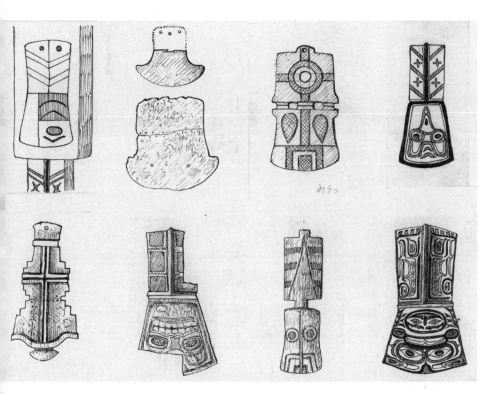

Fig. C.8. Comparative tablets or amulets. By permission of Haffenreffer Museum of Anthropology.

Fig. C.9. Comparative war clubs with figures. By permission of Haffenreffer Museum of Anthropology.

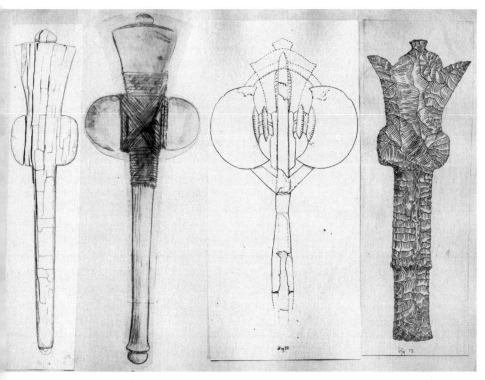

Fig. C.10. Comparative war clubs. By permission of Haffenreffer Museum of Anthropology.

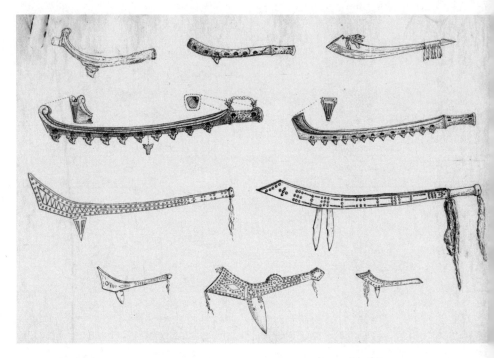

Fig. C.11. Comparative saber clubs. By permission of Haffenreffer Museum of Anthropology.

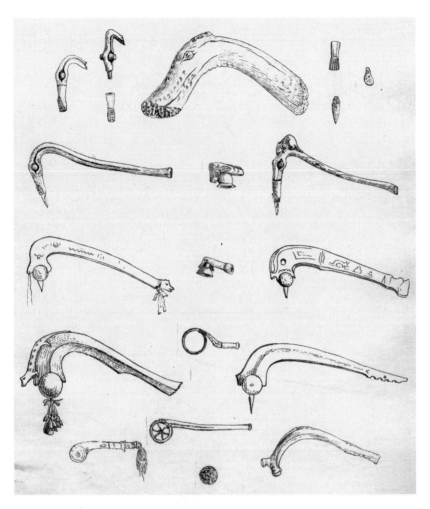

Fig. C.12. Comparative adze handles. By permission of Haffenreffer Museum of Anthropology.

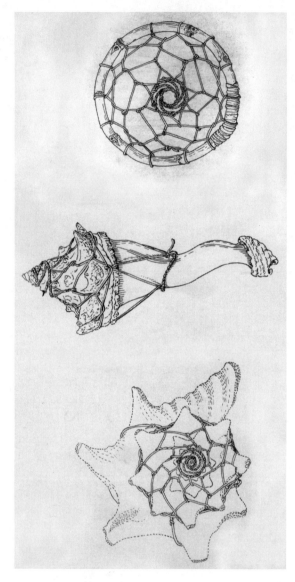

Fig. C.13. Virgin shields. By permission of Haffenreffer
Museum of Anthropology.

Appendix D

Drawings and Sketches

Two institutions house many of the Cushing sketches and illustrations, Brooklyn Museum and the Haffenreffer Museum of Anthropology. It is of interest to note how the material came into the possession of these varied institutions.

Many of the Cushing papers were given by Cushing's wife, Emily, to Stewart Culin after Cushing's death in 1900. At that time Stewart Culin was curator of American and Prehistoric Archaeology, Museum of Archaeology and Paleontology, University of Pennsylvania (now known as University of Pennsylvania Museum of Archaeology and Anthropology). In 1903, Culin took a new position as curator of the newly formed Department of Ethnology, Museum of the Brooklyn Institute of Arts and Sciences (now Brooklyn Museum). He retained the gift of the Cushing sketches and illustrations along with many letters of correspondence from Cushing. Stewart Culin died in 1929, and the following year Brooklyn Museum purchased his collection from his widow. (See Deirdre E. Lawrence and Deborah Wythe, *Guide to the Culin Archival Collection [1996]*.)

Herbert J. Spinden became the new curator at Brooklyn Museum, serving from 1929 until his retirement in 1950. Spinden's widow gave to Professor Smiley of Brown University, who had worked with Spinden, a gift of Spinden's papers, including some Cushing material. The John Hay Library held the collection, and it was later transferred to the Haffenreffer Museum, in 1969.

Original drawings and sketches by Cushing of Key Marco objects bring to light new information concerning some of the extraordinary wooden and shell artifacts. Some of these drawings support the artistic renderings of Wells M. Sawyer. Various sketches give details that are no longer discernible in the continued deterioration of the wooden objects.

In the "Study of bear before casting," Cushing identifies a little-known wooden figure or mask from the Marco site. According to Marion S. Gilliland, two fragments of masks were numbered 40714 and identified "as ears of a bear mask helmet, originally elaborately painted in black, white, and blue." (See Gilliland [1975:85].)

Fig. D.1. "Carved and painted wooden Figure-head of the Pelican." By permission of Haffenreffer Museum of Anthropology.

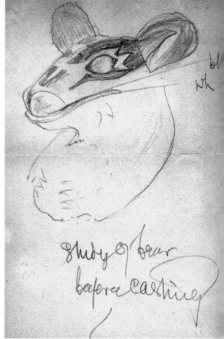

Fig. D.2. "Study of bear before casting." By permission of Haffenreffer Museum of Anthropology.

Fig. D.3. Carved wood saber club. Brooklyn Museum, Culin Archival Collection. Cushing Collection [6.3.005]:871.

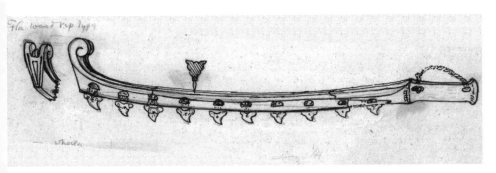

Fig. D.4. "Fla wood rip type." Brooklyn Museum, Culin Archival Collection. Cushing Collection [6.3.005]:872.

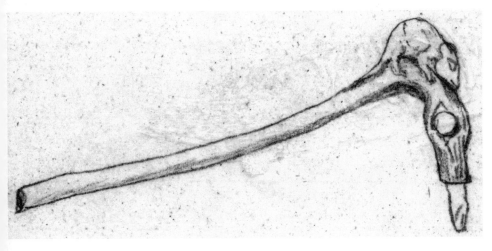

Fig. D.5. Mouse adze handle. Brooklyn Museum, Culin Archival Collection. Cushing Collection [6.3.005]:866.

Fig. D.6. Composite adze handle with socket. Brooklyn Museum, Culin Archival Collection. Cushing Collection [6.3.005]:870.

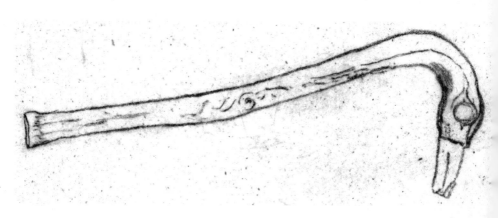

Fig. D.7. Adze handle sketch. Brooklyn Museum, Culin Archival Collection. Cushing Collection [6.3.005]:863.

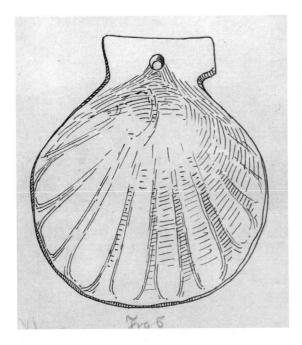

Fig. D.8. Scallop shell gorget. Brooklyn Museum, Culin Archival Collection. Cushing Collection [6.3.017]:222.

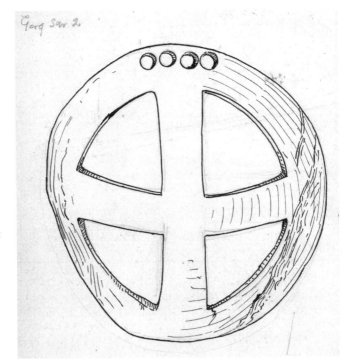

Fig. D.9. Shell gorget with four cardinal quadrants. Brooklyn Museum, Culin Archival Collection. Cushing Collection [6.3.018]:370.

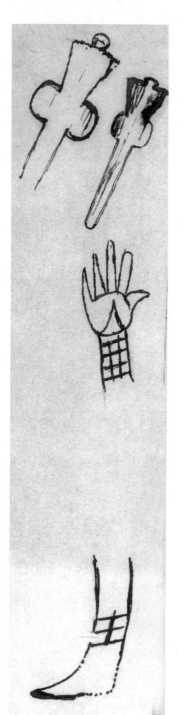

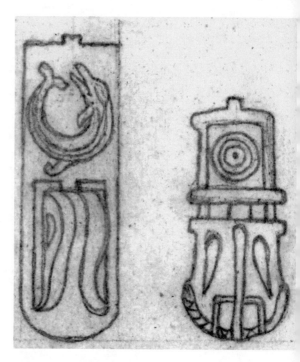

Fig. D.11. Decorated wooden amulets. Brooklyn Museum, Culin Archival Collection. Cushing Collection [6.3.015]:763.

Fig. D.10. Foot, hand, and club sketches. Brooklyn Museum, Culin Archival Collection. Cushing Collection [6.3.034]:A042.

Fig. D.12. Pottery fish mask. Brooklyn Museum, Culin Archival Collection. Cushing Collection [6.3.034]:A074.

Fig. D.13. Wooden amulet with cardinal quadrants. Brooklyn Museum, Culin Archival Collection. Cushing Collection [6.3.015]:816.

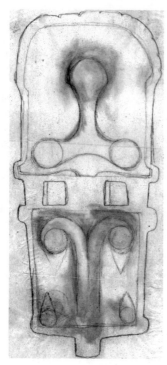

Fig. D.14. Wooden amulet. Brooklyn Museum, Culin Archival Collection. Cushing Collection [6.3.015]:764.

Fig. D.15. Deer mask sketch, view 1. Brooklyn Museum, Culin Archival Collection. Cushing Collection [6.3.010]:442.

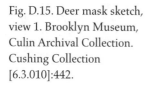

Fig. D.16. Deer mask sketch, view 2. Brooklyn Museum, Culin Archival Collection. Cushing Collection [6.3.010]:121.

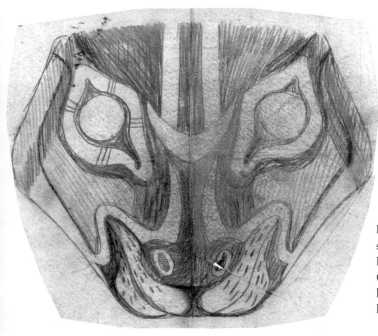

Fig. D.17. Deer mask sketch, view 3. Brooklyn Museum, Culin Archival Collection. Cushing Collection [6.3.010]:119.

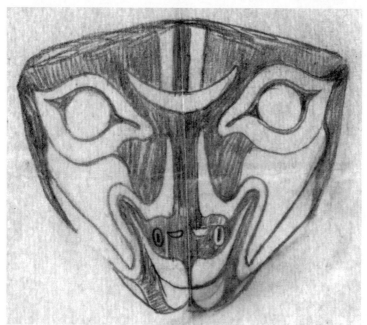

Fig. D.18. Deer mask sketch, view 4. Brooklyn Museum, Culin Archival Collection. Cushing Collection [6.3.010]:128.

Fig. D.19. Deer mask sketch, view 5. Brooklyn Museum, Culin Archival Collection. Cushing Collection [6.3.010]:120.

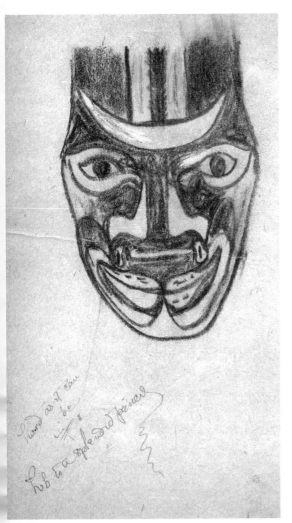

Fig. D.20. Deer mask sketch with pencil comment. Brooklyn Museum, Culin Archival Collection. Cushing Collection [6.3.010]:127.

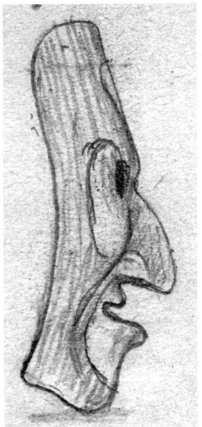

Fig. D.21. Mask study, side view. Brooklyn Museum, Culin Archival Collection. Cushing Collection [6.3.010]:318.

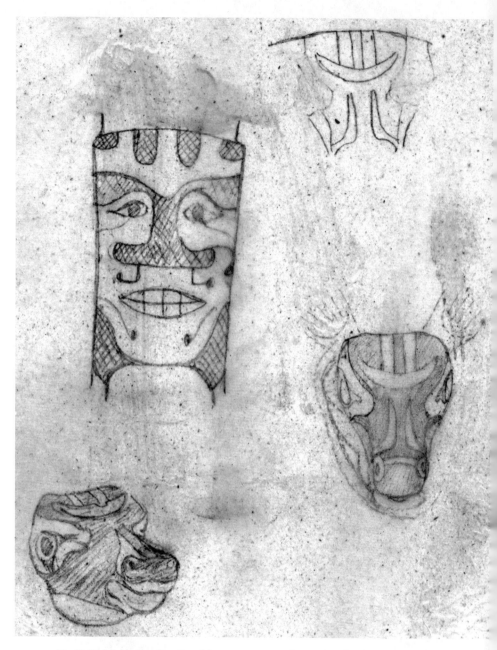

Fig. D.22. Mask sketches. Brooklyn Museum, Culin Archival Collection. Cushing Collection [6.3.010]:184.

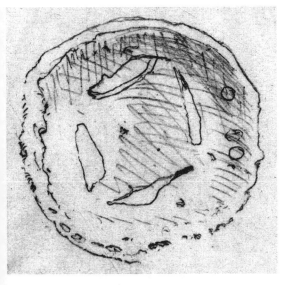

Fig. D.23. Gorget with holes for hanging. Brooklyn Museum, Culin Archival Collection. Cushing Collection [6.3.018]:66.

Fig. D.24. Key Marco painted shell dancer sketch. Brooklyn Museum, Culin Archival Collection. Cushing Collection [6.3.026]:122.

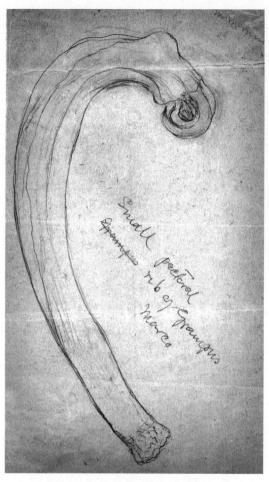

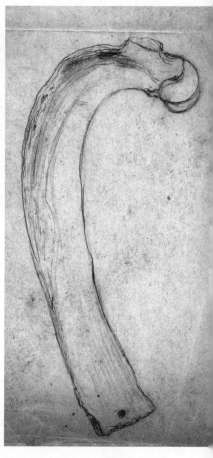

Fig. D.25. Whale bone "Small pectoral." Brooklyn Museum, Culin Archival Collection. Cushing Collection [6.3.005]:326.

Fig. D.26. Whale rib bone with hole. Brooklyn Museum, Culin Archival Collection. Cushing Collection [6.3.005]:328.

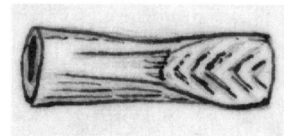

Fig. D.27. Carved socket. Brooklyn Museum, Culin Archival Collection. Cushing Collection [6.3.012]:754.

Fig. D.28. Ear ornament study. Brooklyn Museum, Culin Archival Collection. Cushing Collection [6.3.009]:780–95.

Fig. D.29. Ear ornament. Brooklyn Museum, Culin Archival Collection. Cushing Collection [6.3.009]:707.

Fig. D.30. Vertebrae fetish study. Brooklyn Museum, Culin Archival Collection. Cushing Collection [6.3.012]:705.

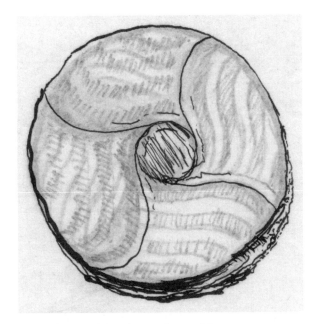

Fig. D.31. Carved vertebra study. Brooklyn Museum,
Culin Archival Collection. Cushing Collection
[6.3.009]:767.

Notes

Chapter 1. Adventure and Initial Exploration

1. See Cushing, journal dated May 20, 1895 (1895c).

2. See Hodge-Cushing Collection, journal dated May 28, 1895, MS.6.PHE.1.2. All excerpts from the Hodge-Cushing collection are courtesy of Southwest Museum, Los Angeles, California.

3. Thomas Hovenden (1840–95), an Irish-American painter, received acclaim for his sensitive portrayals of American historical events. The Cushings stayed with Hovenden in early May of 1895 at Plymouth Meeting in Montgomery County, Pennsylvania, prior to the initial trip to Florida (letter from Cushing to Stewart Culin, Brooklyn Museum Archives, Culin Archival Collection, Cushing Collection [6.1.003]: correspondence, 1895).

4. *Tennison* was Cushing's wife's middle name. He referred to her as such three times in these journals.

5. William H. Rau was a successful expedition photographer from the mid-1870s through the 1880s. In 1895 he moved his studio to a fashionable section of Philadelphia and prospered as a portraitist (University of Pennsylvania, Document Archives). Cushing circulated in the highest echelon of Philadelphia society, also apparent from the mention of the Wanamaker's, an elite clothing establishment.

6. Free transportation as an inducement to Florida was a common practice to encourage land purchase and settlement of the Disston Companies' real estate ventures. A pamphlet produced by the Gulf Coast Land Company states "free transportation available on application whether you desire to invest or influence capital or emigration" (*The World's Sanitarium* 1885). The land developers saw an opportunity in Cushing's explorations as further enticement to Florida lands. It would enhance interest in their land holdings and promote sales.

7. Col. James M. Kreamer, an engineer, was affiliated with Hamilton Disston and his Florida Land and Improvement Company. The politically savvy Disston had purchased some four million acres of land for 25 cents an acre in 1882 and rescued Florida from bankruptcy. The young entrepreneur had big plans for real estate development and established many land companies throughout Florida, but he died

suddenly on April 30, 1896 (Knetsch 1998). Kreamer, with other investors, continued to promote development of the lands.

8. Fort Thompson, established ca. 1839, was located southwest of Lake Okeechobee during the Seminole Wars. Fort Thompson remained a Confederate interior fort and served as a cattle roundup and assisted blockade runners (Dibble 1999). After the Civil War, Fort Thompson was an established village (Fritz 1963:17). The great mound beyond Fort Thompson most likely referred to the imposing mounds of Mound Key further down the Caloosahatchee River on Estero Bay.

9. Emily Tennison Magill married Cushing in Washington, D.C., on July 10, 1883, when he returned briefly to Washington during his prolonged ethnographic study of the Zuni. Her given name, Emily, used in all other references, was never used by Cushing in any of these diaries; he always called her Emalie. A possible reason comes from a letter written in 1884 to Cushing from his Zuni brother, Palowahtiwa. The phonetic spelling and pronunciation of Emily in the letter is Em-a-li-a. See Green 1990:328.

10. Robert Stewart Culin was appointed in 1892 as director of the University of Pennsylvania Museum of Archaeology and Paleontology. He became the curator in 1899. Culin and Cushing, as well as their wives, were good friends throughout the years. They collaborated on various projects (Lawrence and Wythe 1996:13–17).

11. Dr. William Pepper established a teaching school of medicine at the University of Pennsylvania. He was also president of the Archaeological Department at the University of Pennsylvania and Cushing's personal physician.

12. Daniel G. Brinton was the first professor of anthropology at the University of Pennsylvania. He was affiliated with the American Philosophical Society and was president of the American Association for Advancement of Science, among other affiliations. Brinton led the discussion following Cushing's presentation of his preliminary report on ancient key-dwellers at the 1896 Proceedings of the American Philosophical Society.

13. The Honorable Charles P. Daly was the president of the American Geographical Society and corresponded with Cushing in the 1880s concerning Zuni manuscripts. Cushing wrote and illustrated articles for the society to publish (letter dated September 9, 1886, Cushing to Daly, Hodge-Cushing Collection, MS.6.BOE.1.15).

14. Cushing's family moved to Barre Center, Orleans County, New York, when he was three years old. Many of Cushing's relatives lived in Barre Center and nearby Albion, including Cushing's brother Enos, a dentist. When Cushing was only seventeen years old, he sent a paper about the antiquities of Orleans County to the Smithsonian Institution. It was published in the Annual Report that year (Brandes 1965:7–9).

15. Cushing thoroughly enjoyed himself on his trip southward. His characterizations of the other passengers were amusing. This was a person who now attained a prominent status in America's Victorian society and was publicly recognized as one of the preeminent ethnologists.

16. See Gilliland 1989:27.

17. Cushing gave a detailed account of his Florida explorations in a presentation to the American Philosophical Society on November 6, 1896. That preliminary report, *Exploration of Ancient Key-Dweller Remains on the Gulf Coast of Florida*, was published the following year. The report was recently republished.

18. Captain John Smith, a Norwegian sailor, was the first permanent resident of Pine Island, in 1873. When developers arrived in 1885, Smith built and rented rowboats for fishermen and became a guide for the rich visitors. His sons, John Jr. and Frank, also became captains and guides. Cushing first hired Captain Smith Sr.; later, on June 10, he hired young Johnny, Smith's son, to assist with the remainder of his explorations in 1895 (Brooks and Crabtree 1982:93).

19. The first site Cushing explored in his initial reconnaissance he first called Cashe's Key or Casey's Key. He decided in his unpublished manuscript to call the site Gardens Key, perhaps because of all the evidence he saw of ancient gardens: digging tools and basins that appeared to have been used as garden plats. The key impressed him with its artificial origin and structural features. He discussed this key at length, without naming it, in the beginning of his presentation at the Proceedings of the American Philosophical Society (Cushing 1897b:331–35). In Cushing's manuscript (1896e), he further described the key as the "northernmost of the so-called Barras Island" in the middle of Pine Island Sound channel, two miles southwestwardly from Patricio Key and approximately one and half miles eastward of Useppa Island.

20. The old fishing stations on Useppa Island, now pelican rookeries, planted in Cushing's mind visions of the aboriginal people's "fish-drives and fish-pools" (Cushing 1897b:336–37). The Spanish were Cubans that occupied Useppa in the early 1890s. See Pearse (1954). Other references refer to the Spanish-Indians on Useppa, see Fritz 1963 and Edic 1996.

21. Josselyn's Key (8LL32), also visited the early morning of May 30, 1895, possessed the special feature of the flat, one-half-acre central court surrounded by five very high mounds divided by deep-cut channels. Cushing's map clearly details these topographic features.

22. Beatties [aka Battey's] Landing (8LL33) is the site of Pineland on Pine Island. It was named after William Batty of Levy County, who purchased 142 acres of Pine Island on April 10, 1885 (Jordan 1982:8). This was Cushing's initial visit, where he sketched one map of the high mounds. He revisited the site on June 10, 1895, drawing an explicit map of this area, including the main canal that is of present interest for purchase and preservation. Cushing also shows additional canoe ways and branch canals on his map. Lateral canals were discussed by George M. Luer and Ryan J. Wheeler in their article "How the Pine Island Canal Worked: Topography, Hydraulics, and Engineering" (1997). Cushing actually described traces of wood posts as possible gates at the mouth of one branch canal that correspond with anomalies and the hypothesis of "water-control structures" in Luer and Wheeler's survey (Cushing 1896e).

23. Captain Edgar A. Whiteside, a prominent resident of St. James City, affiliated with the New England developers (including Kreamer) that came to Pine Island in

1885. Whiteside built a general store up on pilings that also served as post office and warehouse (Brooks and Crabtree 1982:93). He told Cushing he destroyed some of the shell mounds to make roads.

24. Homesteaders settled on Sanibel Island in the 1880s. Rev. George Barnes built a church on Sanibel, with a high cross that sailors could see. He also built the first resort hotel on Sanibel, called "The Sisters" (Fritz 1963:89–90 and Pearse 1954:13–14). Cushing was confused, Barnes had two daughters and a son, not three daughters. One daughter married Edward Duncan (Anholt 1998:23, 43–44).

25. Cushing described Capt. Sam Ellis's Place in his report (Cushing 1896e:346–47). Ellis Bay is now called Tarpon Bay within the J. N. "Ding" Darling National Wildlife Refuge. Sam Ellis lived with his wife, who was part Indian, on the south shore (Anholt 1998:29). In Cushing's unpublished manuscript (1896e) he depicted in detail the quaint thatched palmetto shacks that Mrs. Ellis kept "scrupulously clean." The ever observant Cushing described explicitly the construction, furnishings, utensils, and even bundles of herbs and seeds in the main hut, where he spent the night. Cushing was moved by the generosity and kindness of the Ellis family, as each secretly, even little Sam, gave his or her most prized possession to Cushing. This was a small cache of coffee shells. Cushing in his Proceedings report, manuscript, and diary also mentioned a burial mound he excavated on northeast Sanibel Island next to Ellis's Place.

26. In 1896, Maj. George R. Shultz operated one of the early telegraph cable offices at Punta Rassa that reached down the coast of southwest Florida, Key West, and on to Cuba. His cable station, the "Barracks," was actually Fort Dulaney, built during the Seminole Wars (Pearse 1954:6–8). There he also often housed tarpon sportsmen, "strickly stag" (Fritz 1963:89).

27. Frank Johnson and his wife, "Molly," settled on Mound Key in the 1870s. They received a deed to the island, signed by President Benjamin Harrison, in 1891. Molly was known as an herbal healer and midwife (Edic 1996:67).

28. Mound Key, or Johnson's Key (8LL2), located in Estero Bay investigations, produced numerous collections dating from Caloosahatchee I–V (ca. 500 B.C.–A.D. 1750), as well as Spanish artifacts. Many archaeologists consider this site the possible location of Calos, the residence of Carlos, chief of the Calusa (Mitchem 1999:21–22). C. B. Moore disputes Cushing's observation of the principal mound on the key in his 1900 address to the Academy of Natural Sciences. Cushing took "5–6" photographs of this site (Wheeler 2000:2). Cushing described in detail in his unpublished manuscript (1896e) his observations of the mounds, canals and lagoons. When the Pepper-Hearst Expedition revisited the site in 1896, Wells Sawyer drew a map showing the position of the mounds and canals. Moore's drawing of this mound in Mitchem (1999:185) does not appear to be anything like the mound that Cushing described and Sawyer sketched, both of which are remarkably similar to a detailed map and profile drawn by Corbett Torrence in 1994. See Wheeler 2000:5 and the Florida State Park brochure Mound Key State Archaeological Site.

29. Hamilton Disston's developers arrived in the late 1880s amid the protests of

the earlier settlers. Captain Large must have been part of that contingent, since Cushing was given a letter of introduction from Kreamer. The Naples canal, of aboriginal construction, was drawn on the first plat map of 1887. It was described "as being fifty feet wide" (Tebeau 1957:165–66). Although other early descriptions of the canal vary in width and depth and it was an "object of wonder" for early visitors, it is no longer extant. George Luer described the Naples Canal (8CR59) as approximately 1.3 km (0.8 mi) and connecting Naples Bay with the Gulf of Mexico (Luer 1998).

30. Cushing continued throughout these Florida journals to comment on his theory of Caribbean origin of native emigration into Florida.

31. These initial observations written in the diary of 1895 prior to the Pepper-Hearst Expedition to Key Marco are very comparable to Sawyer's explicit topographic map of 1896, Plate 30 (Cushing 1897b). Cushing's remarks support his keen ability of observation.

32. Cushing's first attempt to rid the muck pond of water was a turf dam. George Gause's idea of a trough was utilized in the 1896 field season.

33. Cushing explored the St. James City mound sites, many that Whiteside acknowledged he destroyed. This exploration was described in detail in his later manuscript (1896e).

34. Cushing described Alexander Montgomery as a capable, well-educated Scotchman. He engaged his help, as well as that of young John Smith, to reexamine many of the keys and islands because of his newly acquired understanding of the artificial key-dweller landscape after his visit to Key Marco (Cushing 1896e).

35. George H. Kirk and Captain Rhoads were vegetable farmers at Battey's Place north of St. James City (Jordan 1982:102). The detailed map of Beatties (Battey's) Place showed distinctively the archaeological features of the canals, lake, and high and truncated mounds of what is now called Pineland. Cushing's map indicated a huge complex aboriginal settlement. A cypress figurehead of a crane or other long-beaked waterbird was recovered from the mud in 1971. This low area is now drained. A complete description and study of the figurehead is in Faces and Figureheads: The Masks of Prehistoric South Florida by Merald R. Clark (1995).

36. Cushing drew a detailed, "laboriously" sketched map of Demorey's Key from the top of a tree on June 10, 1895, including the "high square mound" that he indicated on the map and described in his report (Cushing 1897b:338–41). Two severe documented freezes hit Florida in the winter of 1894–95, devastating many of the fruit groves and other native vegetation, as the freezes extended deep into southern Florida (Florida Historical Society 1909:26). Cushing mentioned in his manuscript (1896e) that much of the foliage was denuded from the tops of the trees. This factor no doubt aided him in his visual survey. In 1896, the Pepper-Hearst Expedition photographed and tested the site, including the conch shell wall, and ascertained it was of prehistoric construction. After Cushing's death this became a controversial issue.

37. Cushing was asked to give a lecture at Whiteside's store about his Zuni adventures. All the male settlers from the surrounding area came to listen to Cushing, and

this gave him the opportunity to question many about the landscape farther inland to help confirm his formulating hypothesis. Cushing writes a lengthy description of this evening (1896e).

Chapter 2. Excavations amid Anxiety

1. Members of the expedition, besides Cushing and his wife, from Washington, D.C., were Wells M. Sawyer, volunteer artist and photographer from the United States Geological Survey, and Carl F. W. Bergmann, a curator from the U.S. National Museum. Irving Sayford, a volunteer from Harrisburg, Pennsylvania, acted as field secretary.

2. An advertisement dated December 1886 in *The South* about the Tarpon Springs Hotel delineated the city's many desirable attributes. Cushing mentioned Cheyney and Marvin in his American Philosophical Society preliminary report of November 6, 1896, (Cushing 1897e:352).

John K. Cheyney was from Philadelphia and a business associate of Hamilton Disston, and his large real estate companies. Cheyney established the first sponge business in Tarpon Springs in 1891, The Anclote and Rock Island Sponge Company. He became the President of the Lake Butler Villa Company, a Disston enterprise, in 1891, upon the death of Anson P. K. Safford. See references at the Tarpon Springs Area Historical Society. *The Florida Gazetteer and Business Directory of 1895* listed H. G. Marvin as proprietor of the Tarpon Springs Hotel.

3. Map drawn by Jonathan B. Walton in 1883, showed the Indian Mound. Walton was a surveyor brought in by Hamilton Disston to plan the town. See references at the Tarpon Springs Area Historical Society.

4. Letter from Wells Sawyer to his fiancée, Kathleen, dated Sunday, December 22, 1895, "Our boat has arrived and next week we will probably be bound for the south tho not until after Christmas" (Sawyer 1895–96).

5. Letter from Wells Sawyer to Kathleen, dated Tarpon Springs, Fla. Dec. 11, 1895. "We have accomplished a good deal today, we began after breakfast and have been working all day opening a mound a short distance from the house. We have found some beautiful and stunning fragments of pottery with very fine designs on them. They are like South American designs and are much more beautiful than any northern work I have ever seen. There is no doubt that the archaeological side of the expedition will be a success" (Sawyer 1895–96).

6. Letter from Wells Sawyer to Kathleen, postmarked December 20 from Camp Hope, located about 9 miles north of the Safford Mound site. "Today we began opening a mound near here, it is small but some good things are promised. As yet our boat has not arrived" (Sawyer 1895–96).

7. A sharpie is a long, narrow, flat-bottomed boat with a triangular sail.

8. Cushing was reluctant to give interviews, because of his agreement with expedition benefactor Mrs. Phoebe Hearst, who expected first publicity and release of expedition news. Apparently, by February, Cushing relented and held a news session with correspondents. Several newspapers wrote on the exciting Tarpon Springs dis-

coveries and published columns in their local newspapers. February 2, 1896, *Times* (Jacksonville, Florida) headlines read: "Curious Finds by Cushing; The Explorer Delving into Florida Indian Mounds; Scores of Grinning Skulls; and some skeletons in a fair state of preservation" (*Citizen* [Jacksonville, Fla.], February 2, 1896, "Relics of a By-Gone Race; Frank Hamilton Cushing at Work at Tarpon Springs; Rare Discoveries in Ethnology" *Post* [Washington, D.C.], February 3, 1896, "Amid Pots and Skulls; Labors of Washington Scientists in Florida" (Bureau of American Ethnology, Smithsonian Institution no. 1840).

9. Cushing wrote of the human remains from the Safford and Hope Mounds in his article, "Scarred Skulls of Florida."

Of the better preserved skulls of adults among these remains, about nine in fifty were of special interest as exhibiting crest-ridges; that is, on each, extending from the front apex backwardly and divergingly along either side of the coronal and to the parietal regions was a slight but very marked and regular ridge formed by a papuloid growth of bone, which seemed to have resulted from the cicatrization of the scalp, caused by the shaving or the removal otherwise of hair from the sides of the head and by the singeing or cauterization of the scalp along the lines indicated, so as, by preventing growth, to sharply define the lateral boundaries of the hairy crests thus left.(1897c:17–18)

Cushing continued explanation that the "jay or kingfisher (crested-bird)" in some tribes denoted the warrior class.

10. Richie, White, and Styles were locals Cushing employed to help with his excavations. "Richie" was William A. M. Richey, the son of Captain Aaron M. Richey, who docked his schooner in what became Port Richey. They moved to Tarpon Springs in 1892 to be near a doctor, whereupon Captain Richey served a term as mayor (Dill 1986). Louis Styles was the son of Lily Styles, who first came to Tarpon Springs in the 1880s and worked as a housekeeper for the prominent Safford family (Tarpon Springs Area Historical Society).

11. Cushing's investigation of the Safford Mound continued for another month, resulting in numerous additional finds. The bound catalogs, First Draft Catalogue Vol. 1 and vol. 2, at the National Anthropological Archives, were the drafts Cushing was cataloging on January 22. Vol. 1, Tarpon Springs, Florida, has 146 pages with 271 entries; Hope Mound entries begin numbering at 275. Numerous artifacts, including the caches of pots discovered in the Safford Mound after that date, are those entries listed in the back of vol. 2, as add-ons, beginning with object number 438. In these catalogs Cushing made additional notes of important objects for study and the association of the artifacts, as well as sketches (Cushing 1896c). He put Sayford to work at copying both catalogs on the voyage to Marco. Those copies reside at the University of Pennsylvania Museum of Archaeology and Anthropology.

12. Sawyer took many photographs of the Safford Mound site. This photograph with a view to the north confirmed the site of the Safford Mound on what was Eagle Street (Glenn 1996, photographic lot 2, Fla 127). The sawgrass ponds in the background were drawn on the Walton map, and African-American churches are the

buildings to the left in the photograph. The tall large pines are the same trees described by S. T. Walker in his diagram of the Ormond Mound (aka Safford Mound) (1880:398). These tall pines were also drawn on the Wells Sawyer map of the site in a profile that includes the stratigraphy of the burials (Photographic lot 2, 45012B, National Anthropological Archives, Smithsonian Institution).

13. Professor Smeltz was described as a German, and first band leader for the town concerts (Pent 1964:43). Smeltz also owned an oyster farm off a small island and supplied the town with oysters (*Florida West Coast Truth*, February 27, 1897, Tarpon Springs Area Historical Society).

14. These designs were mentioned by Cushing in the American Philosophical Society Proceedings: "small flat-bottomed bowls, decorated by means of etched and carved lines, some of these being maskoidal in character" (Cushing 1897b:353). Cushing described this particular vessel in detail in his manuscript (Cushing 1896e).

15. A letter from Cushing to Pepper dated March 1, 1896, mentioned this letter, and Cushing's appreciation and relief upon receipt of this correspondence (Cushing 1896b).

16. Spring Bayou, one block from the Tarpon Springs Hotel, remains a community focus. Victorian homes built in the 1880s and 1890s surround the deep, round end of the bayou that was described in detail by Walker: "Near the head or end of this bayou is a deep round pond called the 'Boiling Spring' . . . known for miles around, and is said to be of unfathomable depth." Walker described the Safford Mound, then known as the Ormond Mound, and sketched the area, plate 2: "Half a mile to the northeast of this spring is a circular sand mound, built at the foot of a low sand ridge . . . close at hand . . . is a series of shallow ponds, surrounded by marshes." He did some investigation of the mound and sketched with description the burials he excavated and sent to the Smithsonian (S. T. Walker 1880:396–99).

17. Spanish moss was most likely used as a packing material.

18. Cushing's choice of Antonio Gomez as captain proved a good selection, for he was well known as a skilled navigator. Gomez's father was Maximo Antonio Hernandez, guide to Colonel Brooke, and in the 1830s was given a land grant, including Maximo Point, for his services in the Seminole Wars (Pizzo 1968:1–12). Captain Tony lived with his sister in Key West as a child and acquired his sister's husband's name of Gomez. Many years later, descendants of the family changed their name back to Hernandez (Pent 1964:79–82).

19. Nest of pots found on Wells Sawyer's birthday. Sawyer was elated. In his letter of February 1 to Kathleen, he tells about his find: "I made the most splendid find the other day which has been found in Florida and one of a few in America, for the significance of the discovery was tremendous. These were five beautiful pieces of pottery buried together and I got down into the trench to show one of the men how to dig. I grew most interested and dug with zeal right straight to this splendid find as tho it attracted me." Sawyer in another letter: "My dear folks at home, . . . I made a simply stunning discovery in the mound, the best ever made in North America from an ethnologic standpoint for it ties up the links in a chain which hitherto have been

disconnected." There are complete descriptions of the cache in Sawyer's unpublished draft of the expedition. (See letters in Gilliland Collection and draft in Sawyer Collection, P. K. Yonge Library, University of Florida.) Cushing's remark about "drumo" referred to the two drum-shaped vessels in this cache (Cushing 1896c:1116–18a). For more description of the pottery from the Safford Mound, see Bullen, Harris, and Partridge 1970.

20. Sawyer photographed numerous studies of the Safford and Hope Mound artifacts. Cushing described the objects in detail in his catalog (1896c).

21. The "Arena" Cushing mentions most likely refers to a publication for public forum where information and opinions are expressed in an open discourse.

22. Cushing's description fits "pottery cache two" photographs. Included with the long gourd jar and lobed jar, Cushing referred to an olla or large mouth jar, and the "exquisite picked line and curved jar," now known as a Weeden Island Punctated design. Although Cushing does not mention in his diary more than four vessels in the cache, he listed all five in his catalog. Bullen in his report listed the fifth jar as a Swift Creek Complicated Stamped, early variety (Bullen, Harris, and Partridge 1970:106). Sawyer also described cache two in his rough draft catalog (n.d.).

23. The map drawn by Wells Sawyer of the Safford Mound shows three strata of burials, as well as dimensions of the mound site of 128 feet in diameter. The large pine trees are clearly marked on the map and correlate with the north view photograph of large trees and the excavation trench. These large trees were also mentioned, sketched, and labeled "c" and "d" by Walker in his 1879 survey (S. Walker 1880:399).

24. Dr. Thomas K. Reed wintered regularly in Florida and was Jacob Disston's doctor from Philadelphia (letter from Cushing to Disston, dated November 24, 1895, Hodge-Cushing Collection, MS.6.PHE.1.5). He owned a "mosquito boat" named *Floralee* that he raced in the sailing events in Tarpon Springs (Pent 1964:40).

25. Cushing's expenses became overwhelming as he attempted to settle the bills.

26. The totem marks were of particular interest to Cushing. He theorized about the ceramic designs, "this pottery was, however, . . . decorated by punctation—literally by tattooing—not merely, I judged, in imitation of tatooed [*sic*] totemic designs on the persons of those who had made and used it,—but in an effort to veritable transfer or reproduce these designs; so that in studying them I recognized much in regard to the totemic organization, and still more in relation to the mythic concepts of their makers" (Cushing 1896e). Cushing referenced those tattoolike designs to the prints Dr. Goode gave him of paintings of Florida Indians made by John White.

27. Cushing referred to "pile decoration as totemic." Most likely Cushing again referred to the crest or raised ridge concept likened to a jay or kingfisher.

28. Lake Butler is a large freshwater lake due east, some seven miles long and 1.5 miles wide. It is now called Lake Tarpon. Numerous archaeological sites have been recorded around this lake, as well as a large burial mound excavated in 1987.

29. This lengthy letter (figs. 2.11 and 2.12) detailed the collections from the Safford Mound as Cushing tried to impress Dr. Pepper of the importance of the finds,

and how C. B. Moore's collection was comparable only in a very "limited sense." Cushing explained that this collection was "monographic," having few duplicates, and should not be broken. Its significance should be further explored. Cushing feared that as soon as he left, collectors would quickly follow him to scavenge any remains of the site. He also related the numerous difficulties he had encountered with the *Silver Spray* (letter dated February 7, 1896, Hodge-Cushing Collection, MS.6.PHE.1.20).

30. There were 35 plummets recovered from the Safford Mound. Most were of extraordinary workmanship and made of a wide range of materials (Bullen, Harris, and Partridge 1970:102). Wells Sawyer wrote home on letters postmarked Tarpon Springs, January 10, 96, "Today we got a wonderful rock crystal plumbett [*sic*] from this mound, also a couple of other ones. All of them very perfect and beautifully worked." Another letter to dear ones at home: "Today we made wonderful finds. One a rock crystal ornament beautifully wrought into a shape like this only more symmetrical. It was perfectly round and very clear. Some 4 inches long. The boat is ready for us yet we do not sail" (Sawyer 1895–96). In his catalog, Cushing describes this plummet as well as the copper plummet found in near association. "84. Rounded, bobbin shaped highly polished pendant of rock crystal with ornate, slightly flaring termination and at opposite end for suspension unique as to material and workmanship—found with 85 and near 83. Slender, round bodies doubly tapered, sinker shaped pendant of marsive copper highly finished and with rimmed ends at one of which cord attachments are traceable found with 84 & near 83 in easterly central excavation under deep burial 3 ft 7 [inches] to 9 [inches]" (Cushing 1897c). The pendants, or bobbets, were recovered in the northwest border of the mound on February 10, 1896, and listed in the back of the vol. 2 catalog as items 598 through 601.

31. Mrs. Inness was the widow of George Inness, famous American landscape artist, who died in 1894. Apparently, Mrs. Inness and her daughter continued to winter in Tarpon Springs and rent the home of Mrs. Levis on Orange Street, less than a block from the Tarpon Springs Hotel. The son, George Inness Jr., a famous artist in his own right, purchased the home in 1905 from Mrs. Levis and wintered there with his wife, Julia Goodrich Smith Inness, the daughter of Roswell Smith, owner of the Century Publishing Co. of New York. Cushing published several articles about his explorations in these journals. Wells Sawyer, the artist, was overwhelmed with meeting Mrs. Inness and made numerous comments in his letters home. "You know George Inness used to live here in the winter time. Well his widow and little daughter are here now, they are with us at the hotel, tho I have not met her yet. Their cottage is not far away, just across the yard and I have been over to his old studio and have seen his bright green paint daubed all over the edges of his studio frames. There is somewhat of an inspiration in even that, yet I wish the great old man was here now. . . . After his death his old sketches brought $112,000.00, which with what he had made besides left Mrs. Inness very well off."

Sawyer writes from aboard the *Silver Spray*, Anclote River, "Well, Kathleen, there isn't much to write. Mrs. Inness has been very kind to me (Mrs. George Inness). She made me a big bag and a table cover and put a cup and paint rags in. She is a lovely old lady. How glad I am to have met her" (letters from Sawyer to Kathleen dated January 18 and February 16, 1896, Gilliland Collection, P. K. Yonge Library, University of Florida).

32. Work continued on the Safford Mound. Cushing mentioned getting more of the face jar. A portion of the face jar must have been recovered earlier and is described in catalog listing 160. "Small portion of face-vessel showing nose, nostrils, portion of cheek, mouth and chin. (Comp. Misfoeic [Mesoic] death heads). Deep, eastern excavation." This pottery sherd is at the Florida Museum of Natural History, Catalogue No. 101682.

33. The neighborhood of Seaside is now the community of Crystal Beach. There are several recorded sites, including Indian Island, now called Indian Bluff Island.

34. Most of these archaic sites up and down the central Gulf Coast are now inundated by water. Cushing's astute observations of sea level rise are indeed correct. In an early letter of Wells Sawyer, dated December 14, 1895, mention was made of a horseback ride cross country to Sponge Harbor where they "finally reached the kralls [sic] where the sponge vessels discharge their cargoes and you would have been surprised to see the shore, covered with sponges which had been thrown aside. I went into the Gulf with my rubber boots and gathered some flint implements left by the Indians but it was too cold for comfort" (Sawyer 1895–96). The Sponge Harbor location (8PI42), a multicomponent site, needs further reassessment.

35. This must be the third cache of three pots. Sawyer described these in his rough draft catalog: "These groups of pottery occurred on the eighteen inch level and were four in number. . . . three pots with many fragments were found" (Sawyer n.d.).

36. Cushing anticipated departure soon; so he closed the excavations and ordered all aboard the *Silver Spray.*

37. Cushing's problems were indeed not over, now he had to deal with a restless crew, a stuck schooner, and mounting bills. The problems Cushing encountered maneuvering the *Silver Spray* into the Anclote River were not exaggerated and were identified in two surveys prepared for the Hon. R. A. Alger, Secretary of War, by the United States Engineer Office of the Anclote River in 1897. One survey reads, "From station 'Bulkhead,' to Sponge Harbor to Tarpon Springs the river is badly obstructed by sand and shell bars, extending from either side of the river and overlapping, so there is no practical channel."

38. Cushing's tenuous health seemed to correlate with his fortune. When things did not go his way, he invariably became very ill. Dr. Reed prescribed for Cushing calomel triturate. Mercurous chloride was a white, tasteless powder for use as a cathartic or laxative.

39. Sawyer was on leave of absence from the United States Geological Survey office and needed an extension. He really hoped that the outcome of this expedition would be a position at the University Museum. He wrote Kathleen in a letter postmarked Feb. 6, 1896:

The boat is soon to sail and I will of course go with it, but as to my remaining away longer than the first of March I want your real advice. Personally I want to return (Washington) but I hate the work at the Survey. I can never get much promotion there, and there would always be a pretty close sail to get along. . . . I have always wanted to be associated with a great university and the museum would bring me closely in touch with the University of Pennsylvania of which it is a department . . . you can see that in a hundred ways it would be better than being a paleontologic draughtsman in the Survey. Still, Kathleen, you will see how useful I am aside from what I study, I take the photographs, make the sketches, survey the mounds, assist in editing Mr. Cushing's work, and am often in entire charge of the excavation. You see Cushing's health is very poor. He is also very busy so I have been made an assistant in a way. (Gilliland Collection, P. K. Yonge Library, University of Florida)

40. Captain Nathaniel S. Patten owned Patten Sawmill on the wharf area utilized today along the Anclote River. He built three steamboats, *Natstone, Ellen,* and *Joe,* as well as a small barge. He also owned a sponging boat and employed many persons of African-American descent to work for him and live in housing that he built for them in what was called "Patten's Quarters." These workers and their families were highly respected and in great demand in the community (Stoughton 1975:32, 43).

41. Dinghy referred to a small boat pulled behind a larger craft.

42. Murphy's tract of land was located on the south bank of the Anclote River. The map from an original Walton survey of 1884 shows the approximate location of the site to which Cushing referred. Recent investigation prior to residential construction recorded the site (8PI44), a Weeden Island culture period habitation. John Mortimer Murphy was well traveled and an author of numerous hunting and fishing guides. See references at Tarpon Springs Area Historical Society.

43. Bryen Mill was located on the north bank of the Anclote River across from Murphy's as indicated by Cushing and on the Walton map. This site (8PI43) had been recorded as a result of Cushing's sketch map that diagrammed numerous sites in and around Tarpon Springs, but the exact location was unknown.

44. Cushing's worries mounted over bills and not enough funds. After a delightful day out and about exploring, he now became ill upon receiving yet another "bad" bill. Dr. Reed prescribed some type of bromide used as a sedative.

45. Deserters Hill's location is on a high sand dune ridge just southeast of Murphy's. The hill was named for a historic incident that concerned Confederate deserters during the Civil War. Recent surface survey at two new home sites on Deserters Hill recovered numerous chert flakes, as well as a Newnan point. Additional limited shovel tests on the highest point of the ridge more than confirmed Cushing's observations of "abundant chips." The site has been recorded in the Florida Master Site File.

46. The east side of Lake Avoca has not been well documented. One site, 8PI236, recorded is on a bluff some one hundred yards from the northwest end of the lake at

the dead end of Lake Avoca Drive. Artifacts indicated in the report were flakes, a biface, and a sand-tempered plain sherd.

47. On this day Cushing wrote to Dr. Pepper, dismayed that Pepper had not received his vital letters with reports and requests for additional funds, and explanations of justification for the need. The uncertainty of his situation and the worry were making him "painfully ill" and in "wretched health." Cushing assured Dr. Pepper:

> ... let me add that results already are such that I am absolutely determined to see this work through! I send you additional proofs in the new sets of photographs of our later finds; in the statement that the catalogue to date contains six hundred and forty-seven entries each covering from on to twenty or thirty or more specimens; that there are thirteen barrels and thirty-seven large and small boxes and cases securely packed, sealed, numbered, invoiced as to contents and addressed to you at the University of Pennsylvania, and stored in the fire proof bank building of this town, to await the first installment of specimens I shall send up from the South with which to complete a full carload lot and thereby not only secure cheaper rates of transportation but also save delivery by avoidance of transfer en route. . . . I will send you a new report embodying (at least in outline) the earlier reports, and henceforth, as you request send weekly letters however brief, as you request. Mr. Sayford is now copying the first volume and when completed will forward to you together with the invoice, which is detailed and exact. (Cushing 1896b)

Cushing later suspected that someone had purposely delayed his mail to Dr. Pepper to cause him aggravation and problems.

48. The next day Cushing wrote another letter to Dr. Pepper, happy to report that he did not have to make an immediate draw but was able to arrange for funds until Pepper could receive the full reports and approve the necessary additional monies, "of say fifteen hundred dollars ($1,500.00 making in all thirty five hundred dollars $3,500.00) [to] be devoted to this cause." Cushing added a postscript to the letter, "P.S. The mere certainty of departure has added ten percent to my health and vigor! The prints were forgotten last night. I send them now." (letter, Cushing to Pepper, dated February 22, 1896, University of Pennsylvania Museum of Archaeology and Anthropology).

Chapter 3. *Silver Spray* Sails to Key Marco

1. Wells Sawyer's toast characterized the pending expedition with well wishes of health and success (Gilliland 1989:68). His recent excavation experience gave him an appreciation for and wonder of prehistoric peoples and their "nature law." Sawyer's quick grasp of archaeological concepts and methodology from his mentor Cushing should place him historically in the annals of early archaeologists.

2. See Cushing 1897b:355.

3. Collier's "new hotel," Marco Inn, was a two-story expansion of the Collier family residence, which had been built earlier, in 1883. The inn had a parlor, dining

room, bathroom, and twenty sleeping rooms for guests (Tebeau 1957:142). The hotel opened in 1895 and was patronized primarily by wealthy sportsmen who came by yachts, since Marco could be accessed only by boat. (See *Fort Myers Press*, n.d., Collier County Museum and Stone [1996:24].) Capt. William David Collier was the second son of W. T. Collier, the first white settler on Marco Island. W. D. married Margaret McIllvaine, whose family lived on McIllvaine Island, an island composed of shell and built artificially by prehistoric peoples, close to Key Marco. It was totally demolished for shell road building in the early 1920s and 1930s. Margaret, "Maggie," kept a diary and wrote about Cushing's visit on Marco. She died of a miscarriage at age 38, in October of 1896. W. D. lost three of their sons, ages 4, 6, and 8, at sea in 1898, all buried in the Marco Cemetery. More information on the Collier family is archived at the Collier County Museum. W. D. Collier built ships, had a general store, and was the postmaster on Marco, as well as a vegetable grower utilizing the rich muck such as Cushing piled up for him. He shipped vegetables to Florida coastal markets (Beater 1965:85–88).

4. St. James City, located on the tip of Pine Island inside San Carlos Bay, was a major harbor on the shipping and sailing routes. Cushing had stopped there on his initial trip to south Florida in 1895 and had surveyed the gigantic shell city located on Pine Island. This stop was brief and "for mail and for taking in of fuel and water" (Cushing 1897b:355).

5. Cushing hired Captain Smith and his sloop *Florida* on his first exploration trip.

6. The hotel San Carlos, built in 1885, had fifty rooms in anticipation of St. James City becoming a large winter resort (Jordan 1982:11).

7. Wells Sawyer's map of Key Marco clearly indicates the area of Cushing's survey and exploration to the east of the muck pond. Excavations across the modern canal from the Cushing site revealed tightly packed shell platform layers. The original Sawyer map of Key Marco is housed at Brooklyn Museum, Culin Archival Collection [6.3.026]:A173. A comparable copy of the Sawyer map, plate 30, is in Cushing 1897b. Also see Widmer 1996.

8. At the end of this daily journal entry, Cushing revealed his symbolic nature and imagery that he manifested and projected into all prehistoric peoples. Raymond S. Brandes traced Cushing's frail beginnings, which had inevitably resulted in a solitary childhood (Brandes 1965). This early lack of companionship caused Cushing to interact with his natural surroundings and undoubtedly formed his uncanny ability to surmise and visualize the landscape of past inhabitants as well as his aptitude to interpret and recreate artifacts. Cushing ended this day's journal with "siget." Perhaps he meant "sigie or signet"; both can refer to a sign or an omen.

9. Sawyer writes in detail about the pile timbers found in "the court," in his rough unpublished draft of 1904. Under the heading of "constructional timbers etc.," he wrote and referred to photographs:

The largest, and in fact the only large timber found was a log fourteen feet eleven inches long and nine inches in diameter, (pl. A 187/167 B 189/170) which could not be removed owning to its great weight and pulpy condition. Both views show also many of the piles in situ. The large pilefer was notched at the side to receive braces or supports which had been bound to it; these notches show more plainly in the larger view B which was taken from the Eastern end. (Sawyer 1895–96)

Referring to the map, the Court of Pile Dwellers site plan, (1897b: pl. 31), which was actually drawn by Cushing, the location of the sleeper is shown in sections 29, 39, and 40. (See Brooklyn Museum, Culin Archival Collection. Cushing Collection [6.3.026]:A143.)

10. Cushing referred to some of the artifacts recovered as "bone and ivory hairpins." All the hairpins found and recorded are of bone. Some of these are highly polished and look very light as if to be ivory. Sawyer also wrote home about these finds in a letter to Kathleen dated "Silver Spray Marco Ship Channel. Mch. 1–96,": "... we have found really wonderful things—The hair pins are very pretty being of bone and finely wrought." Sawyer sketched in his letter one of the bone pins (Gilliland Collection, P. K. Yonge Library, University of Florida). Very light bone pins are specimens #UM70-19-44/lot 40876 and UM 70-19-45/lot 40876 at the University of Pennsylvania Museum of Archaeology and Anthropology. The Florida Museum of Natural History also has specimens of very light bone pins: A4410, A4399, and A4398.

11. Refers to Wells Sawyer's detailed topographic map of Key Marco. (See Cushing 1897b: pl. 30.; original map housed at Brooklyn Museum, Culin Archival Collection. Cushing Collection [6.3.026]:A173.)

12. A sieve and buckets were purchased most likely to screen small objects from the muck. Many small objects recovered denote the careful excavation.

13. George Gause's diary dates from February 6 to April 29, 1896. See Sawyer Collection, P. K. Yonge Library, University of Florida, also Gilliland 1989.

14. A small wood carving at the University of Pennsylvania Museum of Archaeology and Anthropology, no. 40914, depicts a human figure. (See pl. 71, Gilliland [1975:121].) This is most likely the idol mentioned in Cushing's diary. A recent photograph shows the continued deterioration in the wood apparent even since Gilliland's description of 1975: "a small, three-dimensional human figure. This is rather crudely carved with arms at sides, legs slightly flexed, feet together, square tunic or cloak at the back. It is 10.9 × 4.6 cm." Cushing refers to this figurine in his presentation as "a little wooden doll, representing a round-faced woman wearing a sort of cloak or square tunic" (Cushing 1897b:387). Father Juan Rogel, missionary to the Calusa, described in the 1560s the veneration of idols and a temple or house of idols. Despite Spanish conversions, the Indians in the eighteenth century still maintained their idols (Hann 1991:230–87, 422).

Included in the Cushing file at the National Anthropological Archives are an assemblage of miscellaneous photographs and sketches Cushing compiled to compare the artifacts from Key Marco to other finds in various locations throughout the United States. Two views of a small wooden idol from Appanoose County, Georgia, are in this group (Cushing, MS 1846, National Anthropological Archives, Smithsonian Institution). "Key Marco Types," part of his "thousand-page manuscript," dealt with comparisons. Cushing attempted to demonstrate the significance of his key dweller theory and its far-ranging influence. A wooden idol found in 1921 near Lake Okeechobee was published by J. Walter Fewkes (1928).

15. The superbly carved symbolic button of an angelfish, A5600, is well preserved at the Florida Museum of Natural History. Cushing fully described this in detail: "one superb, little brooch, scarcely more than an inch in width, made of hard wood, in representation of an angle-fish, the round spots on its back inlaid with minute discs of tortoise shell, the bands of the diminutive tail delicately and realistically incised, and the mouth, and a longitudinal eyelet as delicately incut into the lower side" (Cushing 1897b:374).

16. Plate 8 photographed during the excavation shows the troughs in place to drain the water from the water court. Plate 8 listed in Gilliland (1975:9). Cushing's diary mentioned the construction for drainage, but does not say it was Gause's idea. Gause clearly stated his role in this innovative method in his daily journal.

17. See plate 24, "Field photograph of mortar, pestles, and shell in situ" (Gilliland 1975:67).

18. The netting at the Florida Museum of Natural History has been partially and very carefully separated to reveal the fine detail and craftsmanship. A detailed study of the net gauges recovered from the Key Marco site demonstrates their use in net construction (K. J. Walker 1992:296–98).

19. Little Marco was a small settlement area just north of Marco Island that was homesteaded by a few hardy settlers who hunted, fished, and grew produce in the late 1890s and early 1900s. John Weeks was one of two brothers who came to the area after the Civil War. His brother Madison's son Bill was one of the guides who took Lt. Col. C. D. Durnford to the Sand Hill burial site (8CR54), a dune ridge some thirty feet high, prior to going to Key Marco. Durnford and Charles Wilkins were guests at a Naples hotel and decided to go amateur exploring for curiosities. Durnford's trip to the University of Pennsylvania to learn more about his discoveries from Key Marco was the chance meeting with Cushing that set the stage for the Pepper-Hearst Expedition. See Durnford 1895.

20. Cushing tried very hard to preserve the fragile wood specimens. He stated the loss of so many specimens in his American Philosophical Society presentation in 1896: "Unique to archaeology as these things were, it was distressing to feel that even by merely exposing and inspecting them, we were dooming so many of them to destruction, . . . I sought by every means at our disposal to remedy these difficulties . . . ordinary glue, shellac, and silicate of soda, proved to be comparatively ineffective. I wrote to Major Powell, asking for suggestions as to methods for preserving our finds . . . to Doctor Pepper, urging an additional appropriation" (Cushing 1897b:359). In a letter to Stewart Culin dated December 15, 1896, Cushing wrote of a formula he discovered that helped preserve the wood objects. To a gallon of dilute

glycerin and a little alcohol, he added one ounce of carbolic acid. This, he remarked, was the same formula used on cadavers. (Brooklyn Museum, Culin Archival Collection, Cushing Collection, [6.1.004])

21. The theory of "key structure" appeared again and again in Cushing's writings. Throughout his explorations, he analyzed the landscape to substantiate his theory. This concept was also embraced by Sawyer, who understood and with an artist's eye could visualize the lay of the land. In Sawyer's unpublished draft (n.d.), he described many of the sites visited on the return trip to Tarpon Springs from Key Marco.

22. The telegram upset and embarrassed Cushing terribly. In a pointed letter of March 1, 1896, Cushing strongly stated his position: "The discoveries I am now daily making are not only unique but are unparalleled in the annals of American archaeology! They are to this century what the discoveries of the Swiss Lake dwellings were to Europe. In the old muck filled water courts of these sea villages I am finding all the arts of the original inhabitants represented with a completeness never before surpassed even in such finds as those of the cliff dwellers." Cushing boldly stated that if University of Pennsylvania could not come up with the funds, he would find them elsewhere. Furthermore he wrote, "And I fear I must ask that any further communication of the nature of your telegram, involving as that did my personal repute, be sent by sealed letter" (Hodge-Cushing Collection, MS.6.PHE.1.20).

23. John B. Calhoun, from Little Marco, was hired as an excavator. The Calhoun family came to the Marco area in the 1880s, and Calhoun Island was part of the area that comprised Little Marco Settlement, south of Hall Bay. Maggie Collier mentions on March 25 in her diary a Dick Calhoun, who "took the Sharpie from his brother and has gone, very angry" (Collier County Museum).

24. Among the remarkable wood artifacts recovered were several slats of wood carefully shaped with gently pointed ends. Cushing wrote that "various thin, painted slats of wood were found in two or three places. They were so related to one another in each case, that it was evident they had also formed portions of ceremonial head-dresses, for they had been arranged fan-wise as shown by cordage, traces of which could still be seen at their bases" (Cushing 1897b:384). These wood slats have striations, from possibly a shark-tooth tool, and noticeable black markings. Gilliland described these in her book: "Cushing says these originally bore a bird device in black. This is no longer distinguishable, but traces of black paint are still visible. The two in good condition, both numbered 40698, at FMNM, measure 29.7 × 2.4 × .6 cm. and 30.5 × 2.5 × .5 cm" (Gilliland 1975:142). These items have recently been given new accession numbers: A5579 and A5580. On slat number A5580, the image of an open eye is discernible. The open-eye symbol is repeated in different variations in the Key Marco artifacts. Cushing theorized this characteristic art form's cultural origin was southern Florida and the Keys and spread from the Gulf northward into the Mississippi Valley regions (Cushing 1897b:399–407).

25. There are two types of line reels at the Florida Museum of Natural History. On A5825 the cord is still wrapped on the reel. Cushing described a flat reel like

A5691: "That they were designed for deep-sea fishing was indicated by the occurrence of flat reels or spools shaped precisely like fine-toothed combs divested of their inner teeth" (Cushing 1897b:367).

26. Another insight into Cushing's character. Other articles insinuate Cushing was agnostic. In this expedition Cushing, apparently exhausted both physically and mentally, and pushed to the end of his capabilities, turned to God for help and guidance.

27. Frank Barnes was employed by Cushing at Tarpon Springs. His father and mother lived in the Marco area and hunted for a living. W. D. Collier mentioned the Barnes family in an interview: "About 1885 the Barnes Family lived on Grocery Bay near the mouth of Royal Palm Creek" (Beater 1965:87).

28. Several harpoon-type points are in the Key Marco Collection. This specimen, carved of bone, is described in detail by Gilliland as "of definite Eskimo type with perforated butt. It is 7.8 cm. long, .9 cm. in width, the barb being formed by notching one side. It is gently rounded at the perforated end and pointed on the barbed end" (Gilliland 1975:213). This harpoon point was numbered 40613 and now is A4411 (Florida Museum of Natural History).

29. Cushing must have finished the rough draft letter started Sunday, March 1, in reply to Dr. Pepper's abrupt and disturbing telegram.

30. The grouping of "tablets of bone, shell, wood" in this diary entry indicated a type of similarity between the objects. In Cushing's Philosophical Society presentation, all the tablets referred to were of carved wood save one of stone, which he described in detail. There are numerous uniform, small, rectangular turtle-bone objects in the collection that Cushing described as possible sacred gaming pieces or for use "in processes of divination" (Cushing 1897b:377). A shell object of similar size—7.1 × 3.6 cm (pl. 119)—and six other square-cut shell sections are mentioned as having uniform size and shape in Gilliland (1975:187, 201). Some of these may now be classified as net gauges and could be verified by the actual netting from the Marco site, which often ranged 5.5 to 6 cm between the knots. The bone pieces were cut from turtle shell and are noted to have worn edges, "to a smoothness and gloss which would indicate much handling" (Gilliland 1975:217). Worn edges could also be caused from their repeated use as net gauges. The turtle-bone rectangles range in size, predominantly from 4.6 to 6.4 cm. See also Walker 1992:296–98.

31. Cushing discussed the matting found: "Portions of mats, some thick, as though for use as rugs, others enveloping various objects, and others still of shredded bark in strips so thin and flat and closely platted that they might well have served as sails, were frequently discovered . . . naught of them could be preserved" (Cushing 1897b:363).

32. Cushing mentioned evidence, on all the ancient keys, of fish ponds filled in to make vegetable gardens. A practice he noted correlated to linguistic ties of Carib and Timucua that "the same word in both" . . . "signifies not only 'Fish-pond' but also 'Vegetable garden'" (Cushing 1897b:447). Gourds found at the Key Marco site were the first found in an archaeological site in South Florida. These were analyzed and

found to be of two types, the true bottle gourd, *Lagenaria siceraria*, and *Cucurbita* variations. All gourds were thought to be used as net floats, "for in most of the lots there are fragments of Z-twist cord" associated with the gourds. See Cutler (Gilliland 1975:255–56). The *Cucurbita* varieties are edible and both types are possibly cultivated. See also recent research at the Pineland Site Complex in southwest Florida (Marquardt and Walker 2001).

33. George Gause described in detail the Sunday and Monday hunting trip that included Bergmann, Sayford, Clark, Hudson, Barnes, Sawyer, and himself to Royal Palm Hammock and the overnight stay with the Barnes family, in his diary dated March 21 and 22 (Gause 1896).

34. George Elliot Cuthbert came to southwest Florida as an adventurous plume hunter. He acquired enough money from the plume trade to purchase half of Marco Island (McIver 2003:46–53). Captain Cuthbert was mentioned in the March 7 entry in Maggie Collier's diary. "The diggers got a thin board with a strange bird painted on it in black and white. Papa and I went down with Mr. Cushing on Capt. Cuthberts wharf today to see this, & the three masks they had previously dug, very curious. These masks were made of wood, with eyes of shell, the mouth puckered up, and some paint is visible" (Gilliland 1989:80).

35. Cushing noted the three masks found on this day. In his presentation to the Philosophical Society, Cushing does not mention the Northwest Coast in his lengthy comparison and analogy of the masks. When the masks were first recovered, the paint was still vivid, and at first impression perhaps Cushing thought the masks similar to the ethnographic fieldwork of Boas, Jessup, and others along the Northwest Coast in the late 1880s and 1890s (Inverarity 1950:51). Boas discussed face masks of the Northwest where painting and features symbolize or represent an animal (Boas 1927:217–18). The historical accounts of the Calusa and the Franciscans mention wooden masks, "painted in white, red, and black" (Hann 1991:195). A master's thesis study of the prehistoric masks and figureheads of south Florida (Clark 1995:125) confirms the first three masks recovered were most likely those shown in plate 45 of Gilliland (1975:92).

36. The "small dish of stamped black earthen" most likely is the small, shallow bowl Cushing discussed at the end of the American Philosophical Society preliminary report: " . . . only tray shaped vessels, and either shallow or hemispherical and deep, sooty, cooking, or heating bowls of black earthenware, were found. . . . One small, shallow bowl, a fragment of which I exhibited to the Society, has happily been almost completely restored. It contains a quite thick mass of black rubber gum-intermixed with crushed shell and other substance . . ." (Cushing 1897b:448). A photograph of this bowl appears on plate 18j (Gilliland 1975:231) and is described as Biscayne Check Stamp; 11 cm × 8.8 cm × 2.5 cm.

37. See Collier County Museum and Gilliland 1989:80.

38. See Gilliland 1989:106–7.

39. Letter, Cushing to Pepper, dated March 7, 1896, Hodge-Cushing Collection, MS.6.PHE.1.20.

Chapter 4. Confirmation of Reef and Key Theories

1. See Gilliland 1989:93.

2. Apparently this week was spent surveying islands in the Charlotte Harbor and Pine Island Sound area. The Whitesides lived at St. James City, and Emalie visited them in lieu of accompanying the island and key investigations. Captain E. Whiteside was noted to be the principal resident of the city and helpful to Cushing (Cushing 1897b:344).

3. Demorey's Key is rich in archaeological remains. The shell wall expertly photographed by Wells Sawyer was described in detail by both Sawyer and Cushing. Remnants of the shell wall remain today. Cushing describes the site as the most remarkable throughout his entire reconnaissance. "Its elevations formed . . . Plate XXVIII,—an elongated curve five hundred yards in length, . . . the lower end or point of this key, consisted of an imposingly massive and symmetrical sea wall, of conch shells chiefly, ten or twelve feet high, and as level and broad on top as a turnpike. . . . The most remarkable feature of this key was a flat, elongated bench, or truncated pyramid, that crowned the middle elevation" (Cushing 1897b:337–41). Recent scholars have speculated that this feature may have been a ball court. See Wilcox 2000:6.

Demorey's Key was also described in detail by Wells Sawyer in the unpublished rough draft that he termed "A concise statement of the excavations on the West Coast of Florida made in 1895–96 by the Pepper-Hearst Expedition under the late Frank H. Cushing of the Bureau of Ethnology by Wells M. Sawyer—volunteer artist and photographer to the Expedition." Sawyer also mentioned old Spanish vessels found in the muck near the structures, but not in the structures themselves. His written comments concerning Demorey's Key are quoted as written excluding the words crossed out.

Demoreys Key which is situated not far from Weysons Key was next visited here many excellent photographs of the shell mounds were made also a sketch map (Figure [blank]). At the point marked x excavations were made in the muck overlying the shell bottom from which old spanish vessels were recovered in considerable numbers these however were in the muck and not in the structure itself. At the points xx excavations were also made which produced only indian pot shards charcoal and no spanish articles—there excavations were in the canals which extended out into the swamp—on the one hand and developed into graded ways going up to the high mounds on the other. The central feature of the mound was an almost level platform much lower than the high shell mounds on either side. . . . It was one hundred and thirty five feet long and Mr. Cushing has written extensively of this feature and Mr. Clarence Moore has controverted Mr. Cushings statement; not having excavated any part of the shell wall with which the northern side of this platform is faced. . . . The part of the wall which is claimed by Mr. Moore to have deliberately left its course in order to pass around the gumbo limbo tree was in my opinion laid up in line with the rest of the wall. The tree is a gigantic one at the ground as will be seen, has in its growth pushed the wall out of line this is shown particularly well in Fig a where the broadening of the spaces between the shells is shown as the wall reaches this spot. . . . Regarding this structure there is no doubt sufficient grounds presented by Mr. Moore to lead one to question the claim of Mr. Cushing that the wall was of key builder origin. Yet the finding of spanish pottery on the key or adjacent to a portion of the wall would hardly be conclusive. The key has been occupied several times probably it was occupied by the Spaniards at a very early date—possibly it was one of the first to be taken possession of them or they may have stopped there with the Indians. (Sawyer n.d.)

Clarence B. Moore's discussion of this shell wall indicates he did excavate on the base of the shell wall itself.

Although Mr. Cushing seems carefully to have looked into this matter, we believe him to be mistaken in attributing an aboriginal origin to this wall of conch-shells. We four times visited Demorey Key with a force of men to dig. The elongated bench described by Mr. Cushing is a portion of an ordinary aboriginal shell ridge, which seemed to us to have been somewhat flattened to serve as a site for a modern house and garden. In fact, we are informed by "Johnny" Smith, Mr. Cushing's guide, that at the time of his visit to Demorey Key [1895], a house, partly in ruins, occupied a portion of this level space just by the little platform. When we first visited the key (March, 1900), we saw a frame house which must have occupied the older one. This house also had been removed when last we stopped at the key.

The wall of conch-shells . . . extends about 100 feet only on the inner, or eastern side, where it distinctly leaves the straight line to go around a gumbo limbo tree. . . . This alone we think sufficient to prove the comparatively modern origin of the wall. . . . The wall itself seems to have been built by some settler in the present century. . . . We removed portions of the shell wall at various places and dug into the mass of material beyond at the level of the base, finding glass, iron and earthenware, one bit with a glaze. (Mitchem 1999:363–66)

Sawyer defends Cushing's analysis of Demorey's Key and makes important observations of confirmation. Among these comments is the reference to a manuscript in the Havana Public Library concerning an early settlement (Spanish) in this area. He also mentions the character of the high mounds with graded ways that are so distinctive and purely key-dweller structure "that they can not be attributed to the spaniard." Sawyer also mentions the placement of the shells in the wall, some greatly weathered through long periods of exposure, others by "the way of which they are arranged that is with the point of the columella down and the broad forming a facing which shed the water," protecting the shells from water collection in the whorl. Sawyer ends his discussion of Demorey Key claiming, "The photographs fortunately show in excellent detail the part of the wall on which he [Moore] bases his principle claim and the discovery of bottles and [s]poils in the land and the level between the wall and the sea fail to establish the facts that the wall was not there prior to the deposit of these articles" (Sawyer n.d.:100–109).

4. Weyson's Key was also identified by Sawyer and described in detail in his unpublished draft. Sawyer left out the number of figures and plates that he apparently planned to fill in later:

Another place visited was known as Weysons Key, and a similar sketch map made upon it is shown in Fig [blank]. Every feature of the key has been affected only by time for from all appearances the key has never been to any extent under cultivation, it therefore stands as left by its builders save only that the perishable structures have vanished. The central lagoon is surrounded on the south by seven ridges varying from twelve to fifteen feet in height. They converge more than is shown in the sketch map. Beyond there are a few other lower ridges on a platform mound. To the north of these ridges is the great central lagoon. Enclosed corsed and protected by elaborately planned low ridges of shell, to the north of the central water court or lagoon is a curious steep shell structure, shown in section in Fig [blank]—and located on the sketch map at x the sides of this mound are so steep that it is very difficult to ascend; the top of the mound is narrow and has two well defined ridges with a hallow between traversing its entire length on one side there is a lower mound with a level top both of these structures are comparatively small the taller being probably eighteen or twenty feet high by maybe thirty feet in length. The mound rises on one side from the central water court and on the other from a broad nearly level roadway leading off north into the swamp—I regret that the time given to this remarkable Key would not permit of further investigations on my part. Mr Cushing with a party of men dug in the swamp and found the usual evidences of its having been the home of indians—nothing spanish or modern was found. The excavations were hurried and the time spent on this remarkable Key was altogether inadequate to produce more than suggestive results. A decided contribution to American archaeology is made in the mere announcement of this Key. (Sawyer n.d.:96–100)

Sawyer wrote that Demorey's Key was situated not far from Weyson's Key. A probable location of Weyson's Key is Galt Island. This needs further investigation.

5. The term *Teocalli*, used by Cushing, described the shell wall and its resemblance to the skull rows found at Tenochitlán in Mexico City and Chichen Itzá. (Personal correspondence, John Beriault, July 2000.)

6. Cushing remarked that Battey's Landing (8LL33) on Pine Island was approached only by wading at low tide. Captain Kirk and Captain Rhodes worked the land as a vegetable farm. Cushing could easily identify all the key-dweller features there: the canals, mounds, courts, and graded ways. The inner courts were extensive and served for modern gardens, and these were "framed by great shell structures"

with summit mounds that towered up to sixty feet (Cushing 1897b:341). Some of the items collected by Cushing on Battey's Landing were items numbered UM 41219–41222; "a small much worn adze shell—dug in mouth of great canal, pair of worked columellae and one finished triton shell ear pendant—from the canal area, miscellaneous lot of pot sherds and burial remains in Great Sand Mound, shell and marl cement (partially fossilized) in ancient key foundation" (Gilliland research notes, Florida Museum of Natural History).

7. This entry in the journal indicates another notebook. Mention of additional sketches and notes in the other journals and his catalogs suggest Cushing's use of field sketches and fieldnotes for more detail. This indicates the possibility that more Cushing material may surface.

8. Letter, Cushing to Pepper, dated April 27, 1896 (Cushing 1896b).

9. Fishermans Key was not mentioned in the Cushing diary, but listed by Gause. The artifacts acquired at this location were of Seminole origin.

10. Egmont Key sits at the entrance to Tampa Bay and just southwest of Mullet Key. A lighthouse was erected in 1848. Egmont and Mullet Keys were reserved for military purposes as early as March 23, 1849. This position was made permanent by executive order on November 29, 1882 (Sarles 1960). Mullet Key was originally made up of six small islands: Mullet, Center Mullet, East Mullet, Hospital, Rattlesnake, and North Mullet.

11. Gumo Alamo was Cushing's term for gum from the *alamo,* Spanish for poplar or cottonwood-type trees. Cushing thought the term "gumbo limbo" vernacular and incorrect. He mentioned this term concerning bolls or pod-type capsules. Gumbo limbo, *Bursera simaruba,* trees have pods. In his American Philosophical report, Cushing referred to gumbo limbo as West Indian birches. Apparently, he decided at the last on the return voyage to secure some of this wood and pods for comparison and use.

12. The quarantine dock and station were established on December 16, 1889, by the Hillsborough County Board of Health (Sarles 1960:19). The dock's location was in the vicinity of the existing dock at Fort De Soto Park.

13. Mullet Key has two recorded sites: located on the North point of Mullet Key, a shell midden site (8PI16), and numerous low midden-type mounds (8PI105) located in the Arrowpoint picnic area. The entire area of Mullet Key is now Fort De Soto Park. One long midden ridge area has been bisected by a road to the boat ramp area. This extends southeasterly into deep growth on the south sector.

14. It seems Cushing wrote in his journal the mouth of Mullet Key when he meant the mouth of the Manatee River. On Thursday, April 30, Cushing's diary entry was very short, but he drew a sketch of a shoreline and labeled it "S.E. Site Manatee River Eroded shell structure Sun rise 30th April 1896" (Culin Archival Collection, Brooklyn Museum, Cushing Collection [6.3.026]). Time allotted indicates that Cushing stopped at Mullet Key in the morning, and because of bad weather, Cushing backtracked some 7 miles to Manatee River for safe harbor, arriv-

ing there about 4 p.m. Cushing stated mouth of the Manatee River in his unpublished manuscript (Cushing 1896e). Sawyer's draft manuscript confirmed Cushing's observations as follows:

> At the mouth of the Manatee River are large shell mounds which have been so cut into by the action of the wind and tide that a perfect section eighteen feet high and several hundred feet long is secured. This is shown in Pl [blank] and represents by the dark portions the line of old habitation levels. that the lower lines were old "canals" such as are shown on the Marco map Pl.[blank] is evidenced by the continuation of the hollows, shown on the face of the section, through the high mound and into the low lands beyond. A sketch of the condition is shown in Fig [blank]. In the cliff face of the section shown in pl [blank] shards and coal were found on each of the dark lines and in one case I dug eighteen inches into the mound along one of the lower levels marked x and found shards and bits of charcoal the entire distance in the spaces between the dark lines. The substance was of shell compound of a great variety of species. Mr. Cushing had holes dug, in the beach, at the foot of the section shown in the plate I did not observe the conditions developed; as I remember however Mr. Cushing said the shell structure was underlaid by a mass of conch shells. This was the most eloquent section seen since it gave in perfect condition a demonstration of the Key builders methods—The sections shows the shell hills on both sides of the lagoon, reaching well back into the land, this lagoon might possibly be made to produce as did the one at Marco; other similar lagoons are to be found on practically all of the shell keys. (Sawyer n.d.)

Cushing and Sawyer described Shaw's Point (8MA7), an extensive mound complex that once existed on the southeast side of the Manatee River. This is now the location of the DeSoto National Memorial. Cushing was well aware of the site because of earlier published reports of Daniel G. Brinton in 1859 and S. T. Walker in 1880. See Schwadron (2002:54–57).

15. The Hog Island site that Cushing regretted passing by on the *Silver Spray*'s return voyage was investigated by C. B. Moore in 1903 (Mitchem 1999:297–98). The site (8PI9) had a burial and temple mound. Few artifacts were recovered. Moore had little patience with sites that did not produce for him abundant finds. Cushing must have known there was a mound present on the island from Walker's surveys (S. T. Walker 1880:399).

16. Under the right circumstances, Cushing's stamina was amazing. His comment concerning Emalie and the crew being worn out after months in the field did not seem to include himself.

17. The Anclote Key Lighthouse was built in 1887 and has undergone restoration (Mohlman 1999). The lighthouse attained recognition in 1999 on the National Register of Historic Places.

18. The Clemsons, wealthy winter residents, built in 1903 the largest three-story home in Tarpon Springs, at the corner of Spring and Grand boulevards. Prior to

building the home they were winter guests at the local hotel (Tarpon Springs Area Historical Society).

19. On May 10, Cushing wrote to Dr. Pepper that they had anchored off Anclote the first of the month and it took four days of "very hard work" to unload the schooner. At last situated again in Tarpon Springs, Cushing was befuddled by new problems with passage, as revealed in this correspondence to Dr. Pepper: "I was thrown into confusion by receiving information that my passes (already granted over the Clydelines) would not on account of heavy travel be available until during the latter part of the month. Therefore having abandoned the ship, I at once sent Sawyer and Bergmann home by rail (Sayford left me some weeks ago) and have since been relabelling and loading the collections on car by myself. This week has been much more arduous than I expected it to be, engrossing every moment; but it was finished yesterday, the car sealed and the bill of lading signed" (letter, Cushing to Pepper, dated May 10, 1896 [Cushing 1896b).

Cushing continued to write concerning the bill of lading, which he enclosed in the letter to guarantee the price quoted previously. Cushing also mentioned the collections shipped; the Tarpon Springs Collection was eleven barrels and thirty-nine boxes, and the Marco Collection was also eleven barrels but with fifty-nine boxes, as well as all the expedition equipment. Cushing had problems with the Sanford rail passes for which he had requested vouchers, more than a month earlier, for the trip home. Although the Clyde steamship people were very courteous, he decided to take the shortest route home by train the following day and hoped to arrive by May 13.

20. Letter, Cushing to Pepper, dated May 13, 1896 (Cushing 1896b).

References

Anholt, Betty
1998 *Sanibel's Story: Voices and Images from Calusa to Incorporation.* Virginia Beach, Va.: Donning.

Baxter, Sylvester
1882 An Aboriginal Pilgrimage. *Century Illustrated Monthly Magazine* 26:526–36.

Beater, Jack
1965 *Tales of South Florida and the Ten Thousand Islands.* Fort Myers: Ace Press.

Boas, Franz
1927 *Primitive Art.* Oslo: H. Aschehoug; reprint, 1955. New York: Dover Publications.

Brandes, Raymond S.
1965 Frank Hamilton Cushing: Pioneer Americanist. Ph.D. diss., University of Arizona. University Microfilms, Ann Arbor.

Brooks, Priscilla, and Caroline Crabtree
1982 *St. James City, Florida: The Early Years.* Detroit: Harlo.

Bullen, Ripley, Donald A. Harris, and William L. Partridge
1970 The Safford Burial Mound, Tarpon Springs, Florida. *Florida Anthropologist* 23:81–118.

Clark, Merald R.
1995 Faces and Figureheads: The Masks of Prehistoric South Florida. Master's thesis, University of Florida.

Collier, Margaret M.
1896 Diary. March 5, 1896–May 26, 1896. Collier County Museum.

Cushing, Frank Hamilton
1886–1896 Correspondence, Hodge-Cushing Collection, Southwest Museum, Los Angeles.
1895a A Preliminary Examination of Aboriginal Remains near Pine Island, Marco, West Florida. *American Naturalist* 30:1132–35.
1895b Hodge-Cushing Collection. MS.6.PHE.2.1, Southwest Museum, Los Angeles.

1895c Journal dated May 20, 1895, MS 97-28, National Anthropological Archives, Smithsonian Institution.

1895–1896 Correspondence concerning Florida expedition, Culin 1896 Archival Collection. Brooklyn Museum.

1896a Article in the *New York Journal,* June 21, 1896.

1896b Correspondence concerning Florida expedition. University of Pennsylvania Museum of Archaeology and Anthropology, Philadelphia.

1896c First Draft Catalogue. Vols. 1 and 2. Tarpon Springs, Florida. MS 2527. National Anthropological Archives, Smithsonian Institution.

1896d Journals 1879–1900. Manuscript 97-28. National Anthropological Archives, Smithsonian Institution.

1896e Untitled Manuscript 2526. National Anthropological Archives, Smithsonian Institution.

1896f *Outlines of Zuñi Creation Myths.* Thirteenth Annual Report, Bureau of Ethnology. Washington, D.C.: USGPO.

1897a Correspondence concerning Florida collection. American Philosophical Society Library, Philadelphia.

1897b Exploration of Ancient Key-Dweller Remains on the Gulf Coast of Florida. *Proceedings of the American Philosophical Society* 35 (153):329–448.

1897c Scarred Skulls of Florida. *American Anthropologist* 10 (1):17–18.

1898 Tomahawk and Calumet, Shield and Gorget. National Anthropological Archives, Smithsonian Institution.

n.d. Key Marco Types. 1844-a, National Anthropological Archives, Smithsonian Institution.

Cutler, Hugh C.

1975 Appendix D: Two Kinds of Gourds from Key Marco. In *The Material Culture of Key Marco, Florida.* Ed. Marion S. Gilliland, 255–56. Gainesville: University Presses of Florida.

Dibble, Ernest F.

1999 Giveaway Forts: Territorial Forts. *Florida Historical Quarterly* 78 (2):207–22.

Dill, Glen

1986 Suncoast Past. *Suncoast News.* September 10.

DuBois, Cora, ed.

1960 *Lowie's Selected Papers in Anthropology.* Berkeley and Los Angeles: University of California Press.

Durnford, C. D.

1895 The Discovery of Aboriginal Netting Rope and Wood Implements in a Mud Deposit in Western Florida. *American Naturalist* 11:1032–39.

Edic, Robert F.

1996 *Fisherfolk of Charlotte Harbor, Florida.* Gainesville: University of Florida Institute of Archaeology and Paleoenvironmental Studies.

Fagan, Brian M.

1995 *Ancient North America: The Archaeology of a Continent.* Rev. ed. London: Thames and Hudson.

Fewkes, Jesse Walter

1924 Preliminary Archaeological Explorations at Weeden Island, Florida. *Smithsonian Miscellaneous Collections* 76 (13):1–26.

1928 Aboriginal Wooden Objects from Southern Florida. *Smithsonian Miscellaneous Collections* 80 (9):1–5.

Fletcher, Alice C.

1900 Memorial address. *American Anthropologist* n.s., 2:368.

Florida Gazetteer and Business Directory. 1895. Tarpon Springs Area Historical Society.

Florida Historical Society

1909 *Makers of America: Florida Edition.* Vol. 1. Atlanta, Ga.: A. B. Caldwell.

Florida West Coast Truth. 1898. News article dated February 27. Tarpon Springs Area Historical Society.

Florida West Coast Truth. 1898. News article dated July 20. Tarpon Springs Area Historical Society.

Fritz, Florence

1963 *Unknown Florida.* Coral Gables, Fla.: University of Miami Press.

Garbarino, Merwyn S.

1977 *Sociocultural Theory in Anthropology: A Short History.* Prospect Heights, Ill.: Waveland Press.

Gause, George W.

1896 Diary dated February 23–April 29. Wells Sawyer Collection, MS 53, P. K. Yonge Library, University of Florida.

Gilliland, Marion S.

1975 *The Material Culture of Key Marco, Florida.* Gainesville: University Presses of Florida.

1989 *Key Marco's Buried Treasure: Archaeology and Adventure in the Nineteenth Century.* Gainesville: University Press of Florida; Florida Museum of Natural History.

Glenn, James R.

1996 *Guide to the National Anthropological Archives, Smithsonian Institution.* Rev. and enl. Washington, D.C.: National Anthropological Archives.

Goggin, John M.

n.d.   The Archeology of the Glades Region, Southern Florida. Department of Special Collections, University of Florida Library.

Green, Jesse, ed.

1979 *Zuñi: Selected Writings of Frank Hamilton Cushing.* Lincoln: University of Nebraska Press.

1990 *Cushing at Zuni: The Correspondence and Journals of Frank Hamilton Cushing, 1879–1884.* Albuquerque: University of New Mexico Press.

Hann, John H., ed. and trans.

1991 *Missions to the Calusa.* Gainesville: University Press of Florida; Florida Museum of Natural History.

Hinsley, Curtis M.

1981 *The Smithsonian and the American Indian.* Washington, D.C.: Smithsonian Institution Press.

1983 Ethnographic Charisma and Scientific Routine. In *Observers Observed,* ed. George W. Stocking Jr., 53–69. Madison: University of Wisconsin Press.

Inverarity, Robert Bruce

1950 *Art of the Northwest Coast Indians.* Berkeley and Los Angeles: University of California Press.

Jacksonville Citizen. 1896. News article dated February 2. BAE, Smithsonian Institute, File no. 1840.

Jacksonville Times. 1896. News article dated February 2. BAE, Smithsonian Institute, File no. 1840.

Jordan, Elaine Blohm

1982 *Pine Island, the Forgotten Island.* Chelsea, Mich.: Bookcrafters.

Knetsch, Joe

1998 Hamilton Disston and the Development of Florida. *Sunland Tribune Journal of the Tampa Historical Society* 24:5–19.

Lawrence, Deirdre E., and Deborah Wythe

1996 *Guide to the Culin Archival Collection.* Brooklyn, N.Y.: Brooklyn Museum.

Luer, George M.

1998 The Naples Canal: A Deep Indian Canoe Canal in Southwestern Florida. *Florida Anthropologist* 51 (1):25–36.

Luer, George M., and Ryan J. Wheeler

1997 How the Pine Island Canal Worked: Topography, Hydraulics, and Engineering. *Florida Anthropologist* 50 (3):115–31.

Marquardt, William H., ed.

1999 *The Archaeology of Useppa Island.* Monograph no. 3. Gainesville: University of Florida Institute of Archaeology and Paleoenvironmental Studies.

Marquardt, William H., and Karen J. Walker

2001 Pineland: A Coastal Wet Site in Southwest Florida. *Enduring Records: The Environmental and Cultural Heritage of Wetlands.* Ed. Barbara A. Purdy. Oakville, Conn.: Oxbow Books.

McGee, R. Jon, and Richard L. Warms

1996 *Anthropological Theory: An Introductory History.* Mountain View, Calif.: Mayfield Publishing Co.

McIver, Stuart B.

2003 *Death in the Everglades.* Gainesville: University Press of Florida.

Milanich, Jerald T.
1994   *Archaeology of Precolumbian Florida*. Gainesville: University Press of Florida.
1995   *Florida Indians and the Invasion from Europe*. Gainesville: University Press of Florida.
2000   Prolific Pioneer or Mound Mauler? *Archaeology* 53 (4):56–58.

Mitchem, Jeffrey M., ed.
1999   *The West and Central Florida Expeditions of Clarence Bloomfield Moore*. Tuscaloosa: University of Alabama Press.

Mohlman, Geoffrey
1999   Anclote Key Lighthouse: Guiding Light to Safe Anchorage. *Florida Historical Quarterly* 78 (2):159–88.

Palmer, Edwin M.
1902   *Palmer's Expert Reporter*. Cincinnati: n.p.

Pearse, Eleanor H. D.
1954   *Florida's Vanishing Era*. Printed in the U.S.A. Copy on file at Museum of the Islands, St. James City, Florida.

Pent, Robert F.
1964   *History of Tarpon Springs*. St. Petersburg, Fla.: Great Outdoors Publishing Company.

Pitman, Benn, and Jerome B. Howard
1903   *The Manual of Phonography*. Cincinnati: Phonographic Institute.

Pizzo, Anthony
1968   *Tampa Town, 1824–1846: Cracker Village with a Latin Accent*. Miami, Fla.: Hurricane House Publishers.

Sanjek, Roger
1990   *Fieldnotes: The Makings of Anthropology*. Ithaca, N.Y.: Cornell University Press.

Sarles, Frank B.
1960   *Historic Site Report on Fort Desoto Park, Pinellas County*. Copy on file at Special Collections, University of South Florida.

Sawyer, Wells M.
1895–96 Correspondence, Marion S. Gilliland Collection, P. K. Yonge Library, University of Florida, Gainesville.
1901   Correspondence dated January 1901. File 1840-b. Bureau of American Ethnology, National Anthropological Archives, Smithsonian Institution.
n.d.   Manuscript. MS 53. P. K. Yonge Library, University of Florida.

Scarry, C. Margaret, and Lee A. Newsom
1992   Archaeobotanical Research in the Calusa Heartland. In *Culture and Environment in the Domain of the Calusa*, 375–401. Ed. William H. Marquardt. Monograph no. 1. Gainesville: University of Florida Institute of Archaeology and Paleoenvironmental Studies.

Schwadron, Margo

1998 *De Soto National Memorial Archaeological Overview and Assessment.* SEAC Accession no. 1324. Tallahassee, Fla.: Southeast Archeological Center.

2002 *Archaeological Investigation of De Soto National Memorial.* SEAC Technical Reports no. 8. Tallahassee, Fla.: Southeast Archaeological Center.

Smith, Samuel D.

1971 Excavations at the Hope Mound, with an addendum to the Safford Mound Report. *Florida Anthropologist* 24 (3):107–34.

The South 31, no. 12(1886):12. New York. Tarpon Springs Area Historical Society.

Stone, Maria

1996 *Dwellers of the Sawgrass and Sand: Natives and Near Natives.* Vol. 2. Naples, Fla.: Stone Enterprises.

Stoughton, Gertrude K.

1975 *Tarpon Springs, Florida: The Early Years.* 2d ed. Tampa, Fla.: Tarpon Springs Area Historical Society.

Tebeau, Charlton W.

1957 *Florida's Last Frontier; The History of Collier County.* Copeland Studies in Florida History. Miami, Fla.: University of Miami Press.

ten Kate, H.F.C.

1900 Memorial address. *American Anthropologist* n.s., 2:768–71.

Trigger, Bruce G.

1989 *A History of Archaeological Thought.* Cambridge: Cambridge University Press.

Tylor, Edward B.

1958 *Primitive Culture.* New York: Harper Torchbooks.

1964 *Researches into the Early History of Mankind and the Development of Civilization.* Ed. Paul Bohannon. Chicago: University of Chicago Press.

Upchurch, Sam B., Pliny Jewell IV, and Eric DeHaven

1992 Stratigraphy of Indian "Mounds" in the Charlotte Harbor Area, Florida: Sea-Level Rise and Paleoenvironments. In *Culture and Environment in the Domain of the Calusa,* ed. William H. Marquardt, 59–103. Monograph no. 1. Gainesville: Institute of Archaeology and Paleoenvironmental Studies, University of Florida.

Walker, Karen J.

1992 The Zooarchaeology of Charlotte Harbor's Prehistoric Maritime Adaptation: Spatial and Temporal Perspectives. In *Culture and Environment in the Domain of the Calusa,* ed. William H. Marquardt, 256–366. Monograph no. 1. Gainesville: Institute of Archaeology and Paleoenvironmental Studies, University of Florida.

Walker, S. T.

1880 Preliminary Explorations among the Indian Mounds in Southern Florida. *Annual Report of the Smithsonian Institution 1879,* 392–413. Washington, D.C.: USGPO.

Washington Post. 1896. News article dated February 3. BAE, Smithsonian Institute, File no. 1840.

Wheeler, Ryan J.

2000   *Treasure of the Calusa: The Johnson/Willcox Collection from Mound Key, Florida.* Tallahassee, Fla.: Rose Printing.

Widmer, Randolph J.

1996   Recent Excavations at the Key Marco Site, 8CR48, Collier County, Florida. *Florida Anthropologist* 49 (1):10–25.

1998   Interim Report on the Archaeological Assessment of the Old Marco Inn Project, 8CR48, Operation 2.

2000   Introduction. Reissue of *Exploration of Ancient Key-Dweller Remains on the Gulf Coast of Florida.* By Frank Hamilton Cushing. Gainesville: University Press of Florida.

Wilcox, David R.

2000   Restoring Authenticity: Judging Frank Hamilton Cushing's Veracity. Paper prepared for Gordon R. Willey Symposium on the History of American Archaeology, 65th annual meeting of Society of American Anthropologists, Philadelphia, April 6.

Williams, Lindsey, and U. S. Cleveland

1993   *Our Fascinating Past: Charlotte Harbor: The Early Years.* Punta Gorda, Fla.: Charlotte Harbor Area Historical Society.

World's Sanitarium, The. 1885. Tarpon Springs Area Historical Society.

Index

Page numbers in italics refer to figures.

Phyllis E. Kolianos is environmental education manager for the Weedon Island Preserve Cultural and Natural History Center.

Brent R. Weisman, associate professor of anthropology at the University of South Florida, Tampa, is the author of *Pioneer in Space and Time: John Mann Goggin and the Development of Florida Archaeology* (UPF 2002) and *Unconquered People: Florida's Seminole and Miccosukee Indians* (UPF 1999).

Ripley P. Bullen Series
Florida Museum of Natural History
Edited by Jerald T. Milanich